GOOD NEWS
FOR TROUBLED TIMES

JOHN C. BRUNT

GOOD NEWS

FOR TROUBLED TIMES

REVIEW AND HERALD® PUBLISHING ASSOCIATION
HAGERSTOWN, MD 21740

Copyright © 1993 by
Review and Herald® Publishing Association

The author assumes full responsibility for the accuracy of all facts and quotations as cited in
this book.

Unless otherwise noted, Bible texts in this book are from the *Holy Bible, New International
Version*. Copyright © 1973, 1978, 1984, International Bible Society. Used by permission of
Zondervan Bible Publishers.

Texts credited to NEB are from *The New English Bible*. © The Delegates of the Oxford
University Press and the Syndics of the Cambridge University Press 1961, 1970. Reprinted by
permission.

Bible texts credited to NRSV are from the New Revised Standard Version of the Bible, copyright
© 1989 by the Division of Christian Education of the National Council of the Churches of Christ
in the U.S.A. Used by permission.

Texts credited to REB are from *The Revised English Bible*. Copyright © Oxford University Press
and Cambridge University Press, 1989. Reprinted by permission.

Bible texts credited to RSV are from the Revised Standard Version of the Bible, copyright ©
1946, 1952, 1971, by the Division of Christian Education of the National Council of the Churches
of Christ in the U.S.A. Used by permission.

This book was
Edited by Richard W. Coffen
Designed by Bill Kirstein
Cover art by Helcio Deslandes
Typeset: 11q/12q Cheltenham

PRINTED IN U.S.A.

99 98 97 96 95 94   10 9 8 7 6 5 4 3 2 1

Library of Congress Cataloging in Publication Data
Brunt, John, 1943—
   Good news for troubled times / John C. Brunt.
       p.   cm.
   1. Bible—Theology—Popular works.   I. Title.
BS543.B685   1994
230'.6732—dc20   93-8814
                                                       CIP

ISBN 0-8280-0696-2

Contents

Introduction

By the time you read this, the headlines of the paper and the lead stories on evening TV news will differ from the ones I read and see today as I write this. But in some ways they probably won't differ all that much. Trouble in the Middle East, famine in Africa, natural disasters in various parts of the world, and economic woes will still have a prominent place in the news. In other words, much of the news will be bad! Times will still be troubled.

This book asserts that even though bad news often dominates the papers and the airwaves, it is good news that prevails. Good news about us. Good news about our world. Good news about God. Good news about our future. It is about good news for troubled times.

Amid the bad news about troubled times that continually bombards us, I hope that you find in this good news for troubled times a reason for courage, comfort, and hope.

CHAPTER 1

Is There a Plan?

My wife and my secretary have something in common. They both dislike the way I keep my desk. Both of them are orderly persons, and I must admit that the top of my desk seldom looks very orderly. What they both fail to realize is that my desk is really organized perfectly—for me. I have a purpose for every one of those stacks of papers and books. The problem is that they would need to read my mind in order to perceive the order.

Many people look at our world—with its wars, suffering, pain, and death—and see no order or plan. Life here appears like the top of my desk appears to my wife and my secretary—a place of total chaos with no overall meaning or purpose.

In the novel *Cat's Cradle*, by Kurt Vonnegut, Jr., an important book comes to light in the course of the story. It is titled *What Can a Thoughtful Man Hope for Mankind on Earth, Given the Experience of the Past Million Years?* The newly discovered book raises great expectations. It has the potential for revealing humankind's future and destiny.

The chief character in Vonnegut's narrative is eager to read it. But when he does, he finds that it doesn't take long. The whole book consists of one word, followed by a period. "Nothing."

What do you think? Is nothing all that thoughtful people can hope for? Is there any meaning and purpose in our world? Is there a plan? Is there an order behind the apparent chaos that so often fills the nightly news?

The best news I've heard is that God *does* have a plan for our world. Behind the often confusing array of chaotic events on this earth is an orderly plan that is moving toward a perfect future. Fortunately, we don't have to read God's mind to perceive this plan. He has revealed it clearly in the Bible. In fact, when we use the Bible as a map or interpretative guide, it not only shows God's plan for our world, but it also gives meaning and purpose to each of us.

The Bible begins with the story of our world's beginning and ends with the story of its restoration. In between, we're able to see God's plan for us and our planet.

The first two chapters of the Bible show us that God created a world that was perfect—free from suffering and evil. Adam and Eve, its first inhabitants, enjoyed fellowship with God in a beautiful garden environment. When God looked at all that He had created, He said that it was very good (see Genesis 1:31).

> *Is there any meaning and purpose in our world? Is there a plan? Is there an order behind the apparent chaos that so often fills the nightly news?*

IS THERE A PLAN?

When we come to the third chapter, however, we find that the first humans' open disobedience and rebellion against God brought evil, pain, suffering, and death into the world. In their attempt to be like God (see Genesis 3:5), they actually separated themselves and their world from Him. Genesis 3 shows that chaos resulted. You see, God created these first humans in His own image (see Genesis 1:27), including the freedom to choose how they would live and whether or not they would obey Him.

Adam's and Eve's rebellion created a dilemma for God. On the one hand, He respected their freedom. He would do absolutely nothing to force their wills. On the other hand, He loved them far too much to let their deadly decision be the last word. Somehow He must provide a way to preserve their freedom and at the same time provide escape from slavery to failure and death.

Because God loved these humans so much, and because He is God, He solved the dilemma. He provided a plan in which He Himself would face the problem of failure and death head-on and provide a way for His people to be restored to His original purpose for them.

The precise details of this plan would not be known for centuries. But God did let His children know that He had a plan. He gave them a promise and told them that if they would trust Him and His promise, they would find rescue and restoration.

God first gave the promise to Adam and Eve. He told them that the serpent that had led them into temptation would eventually be defeated (see Genesis 3:1-5, 15).

He repeated this promise to Abraham when He told him that all the nations of the earth would be blessed through him (see Genesis 22:15-18).

He renewed the promise again and again through the great prophets of Israel, who set forth the beautiful

11

vision of a restored world (see, for example, Isaiah 35 and 65).

The apostle Paul tells us how God actually accomplished the promised plan. After referring to the slavery of sin and separation from God that humans have experienced, Paul says, "But when the time had fully come, God sent his Son, born of a woman, born under law, to redeem those under law, that we might receive the full rights of sons" (Galatians 4:4, 5). In other words, God Himself entered into human history by sending His Son into this world in the person of Jesus of Nazareth to adopt us as God's own children and restore our world.

Through the perfect sinless life, death, and resurrection of Jesus Christ, God did everything that needed to be done to solve the dilemma. When we all stood condemned and alienated from God, He took upon Himself the death that we deserved and simultaneously showed us how destructive sin, disobedience, and rebellion against Him really are (destructive enough to destroy the only perfect person who lived on earth) and how much He loves us (enough to die for us).

> *When we all stood condemned and alienated from God, He took upon Himself the death that we deserved and simultaneously showed us how destructive sin, disobedience, and rebellion against Him really are (destructive enough to destroy the only perfect person who lived on earth) and how much He loves us (enough to die for us).*

An uninformed bystander witnessing the crucifixion of this supposed criminal—Jesus—outside Jerusalem on that fateful day in the first century would have seen simply another episode in the continuing saga of suffering that dominates our world. But with the map of God's Word given us in the Bible, we know that God accomplished His plan for our world and assured its restoration through the sacrifice of Jesus.

This restoration, however, did not happen immediately. After His resurrection, Jesus returned to heaven, from which He had come (see Acts 1:6-11). But before He left, He promised His disciples that He would return to the world again (see John 14:1-3). Two angels repeated His promise to them just after He left. They said, "Men of Galilee, . . . why do you stand here looking into the sky? This same Jesus, who has been taken from you into heaven, will come back in the same way you have seen him go into heaven" (Acts 1:11).

The last book of the Bible, the book of Revelation, describes what will happen to our world when Christ returns. It shows that eventually God will restore the world and create a new heaven and a new earth in which all who have accepted God's plan will live with Him forever. A place with no suffering or death.

From all that we have seen, God's plan has cosmic and universal proportions. But it is also very personal. It is a plan intimately involved with each of our lives. How do we, you and I, fit into this plan?

The reality of failure, alienation, and death is not just a cosmic problem. We all struggle with the question of meaning in our lives. We all recognize a gap between what we are and what we wish we were (we will come back to this in chapter 4), and we all, at least at times,

You are all [children] of God through faith in Christ Jesus (Galatians 3:26, NIV).

13

long for the opportunity to live beyond the few short years that life provides us. The death and resurrection of Jesus Christ not only have worldwide significance, but they also speak directly to us in these very personal issues of life.

According to the Bible, the answer to all these pressing problems of life is found in accepting the free gift of restoration and salvation that God offers us. Nothing we can pay can earn it. Nothing we can achieve can deserve it. God freely offers us the privilege of being adopted as His children through Jesus Christ. This means that we enjoy a new relationship with Him that brings peace, joy, and hope. It also means that we are heirs of His estate, so we look forward to a new earth in which we can live with Him for all eternity.

Now, admittedly, this sounds too simple, but it is true. Simply by putting our trust in Jesus (what the Bible calls faith), believing that He forgives us and accepts us freely (the Bible calls this undeserved generosity grace), we find this new experience.

This good news resounds through the Bible. John says: "For God so loved the world that he gave his one and only Son, that whoever believes in him shall not perish but have eternal life" (John 3:16).

And Paul says, "This righteousness from God comes through faith in Jesus Christ to all who believe. There is no difference, for all have sinned and fall short of the glory of God, and are justified freely by his grace through the redemption that came by Christ Jesus" (Romans 3:22-24).

But once we have accepted God's gift of salvation, where do we go from there? Does it actually make a difference in our lives, and don't *we* have to do something?

IS THERE A PLAN?

This new experience really does make a difference, and it also brings new responsibilities. Paul says to the Christians who lived in the ancient city of Colosse: "We pray this in order that you may live a life worthy of the Lord and may please him in every way: bearing fruit in every good work, growing in the knowledge of God" (Colossians 1:10).

In other words, if we really accept God's gift of grace, we will want to live a life worthy of this God who has loved us enough to die for us. We will want to please Him just as a new bride or groom wants to please her or his spouse.

Fortunately, God hasn't left us in the dark about how to live a life that pleases Him and honors Him in the world. Throughout the Bible, He gives instructions that show us how to live this worthy life.

At the center of those instructions are the Ten Commandments, found in Exodus 20. Christians never attempt to obey God and live according to those commandments in order to be saved. God has already taken care of that. But they do, with the aid of God's Spirit, obey God as an act of thanksgiving because of His free gift of salvation.

Christians also devote their lives to sharing the good news they have found with others and setting the focus of their attention on God (see Colossians 3:1, 2) through prayer, Bible study, and fellowship with other Christians (see Hebrews 10:23-25). This new life in no way makes them immune from suffering, but it does give them the inner strength to endure

God's plan has cosmic and universal proportions. But it is also very personal. It is a plan intimately involved with each of our lives.

and even rejoice in suffering, as Paul shows in Romans 5:3-5.

I hope that by now you can see why I began by calling this plan "good news." The rest of this book will explore the details of this plan. Chapters will be devoted to various aspects of the plan, such as the Bible, Creation, salvation, the future of the world, and what God expects of us. I hope that by the time you have read it through, you will agree that this plan is indeed very good news. But the plan is good news for you only when you accept it and make it your own. If you haven't already done so, let the Bible become your map to lead you to God and His plan for your life.

But can you really trust the Bible? Can a book written so long ago really make sense out of our modern, complex world? The next chapter will explore these questions in more detail.

God hasn't left us in the dark about how to live a life that pleases Him and honors Him in the world. Throughout the Bible, He gives instructions that show us how to live this worthy life.

CHAPTER 2

More Than a Good Book

I'm not the sort of person who enjoys crouching underneath picnic tables. On this particular afternoon, however, my family and I had gathered for lunch in a beautiful park. We were enjoying the day until my wife suddenly yelled "Get down!" and dived beneath the table. She spoke and moved with such authority that we all followed suit!

No sooner had we hit the ground, however, than we started having second thoughts. "Why in the world," we asked my wife, "did you do that?"

"Right over there," she said, "a man is pointing a gun at us."

It was probably foolhardy, but I had to look. When I did, I saw a man shaking his head as he set down a camera with a long lens attached. He'd been trying to take our picture, but my wife had ruined his plan.

Some time after this, our family was enjoying a drive in the mountains when we passed a young boy burning trash beside his house.

"Turn around," my wife said. "That boy's in trouble!"

"He's not in trouble," I replied. "He's just burning trash."

"No, the fire has gotten away from him," she insisted. "He's in trouble. Turn around!"

"Sure," I muttered, "and the man in the park was going to shoot us, too!" But I turned the car around and drove back just in time to see the boy run out of the house with his arms full of blankets.

"Please help!" he yelled.

We grabbed blankets and worked feverishly to put out the fire—the fire that had been spreading toward his house *and* the nearby woods.

"Thank you," the boy told us after the fire had been put out. "Without your help, there's no way I could have saved both the house and the forest."

It all goes to show that sometimes it's hard to know *whom* to trust and *when* to trust. Sometimes my wife is right; sometimes my wife is wrong. Likewise, it seems that *every* authority—parents, government, the church—is sometimes right *and* sometimes wrong.

Are there any exceptions to this? Is there any truly trustworthy authority?

Many Christians believe the Bible to be just such an authority. They look to it for counsel, comfort, and meaning. They see it as being the one sure source of guidance in a perplexing, confusing, and ever-changing world.

At the same time, however, a lot of people wonder whether such an ancient Book can really speak to our postmodern world.

> *A lot of people wonder whether such an ancient Book can really speak to our postmodern world. "It's a good book," they say, "but you can't take it too seriously."*

"It's a good Book," they say, "but you can't take it too seriously."

Should we take the Bible seriously? Is it like my wife—sometimes right and sometimes wrong? Or is it something we can trust *all* the time?

Internal Evidence

One way to answer that question is to see what the Bible claims for itself. Probably the most famous text on this subject is found in 2 Timothy—the book recording Paul's advice to the young minister Timothy.

"But as for you," Paul wrote, "continue in what you have learned and have become convinced of, because you know those from whom you learned it, and how from infancy you have known the holy Scriptures, which are able to make you wise for salvation through faith in Christ Jesus. All Scripture is God-breathed and is useful for teaching, rebuking, correcting and training in righteousness" (2 Timothy 3:14-16).[1]

The Bible, Paul says, "is God-breathed." It is "inspired," we would say. This means that the Bible is not *just* a human document. It is not a collection of *merely* human opinions. No, Paul claims that God actually spoke through human beings—that He breathed His that what they wrote would be a faithful representation of what He wanted to say to us. "Scripture comes from God," Paul says—and that's quite a claim!

In this text, however, Paul makes even more claims for Scripture. It is "useful," he says, "for teaching, rebuking, correcting and training." The Bible, in other words, gives us practical advice as to how we should live. It helps us choose the kind of lifestyle that God knows is best for us.

If that were not enough, Paul *also* says that Scripture

is "able to make us wise for salvation through faith in Jesus Christ." Now, Paul doesn't say the Bible will teach you how to build a computer or send a rocket to the moon. The Bible's not much help when it comes time to figure out your income tax—and Paul doesn't claim that it is.

But Paul does say that the Bible will make you wise for salvation. Scripture, in other words, contains *all* the information anyone needs in order to find eternal life. If there's something you need to know in order to be saved, says Paul, it's in the Bible. Nothing important, nothing vital, has been left out.

Jesus clarifies what this information is in John 5:39, 40. Speaking to the religious leaders of His time, He said, "You diligently study the Scriptures because you think that by them you possess eternal life. These are the Scriptures that testify about me, yet you refuse to come to me to have life."

Here Jesus says that the Scriptures point men and women to Him and that in Him we all can find eternal life. He makes it clear that Scripture is not an end in itself. The goal of Scripture is to point. The Bible points to Jesus and leads us to Him as the source of light.

These claims sound audacious, don't they? They certainly don't leave much room for middle ground! Let's be honest. If something claims to be inspired by God *and* a sure guide to the good life *and* all you need to know in order to be saved, then you can't say, "It's a good book, but not something you should take seriously." If the Bible's claims are

> **If there's something you need to know in order to be saved, it's in the Bible. Nothing important, nothing vital, has been left out.**

true, then it's something we *should* take seriously. But if its claims are *not* true, then it's hardly a very good book! No, if the Bible isn't what it says it is, it is deceptive—or even downright dangerous!

So how can we tell whether the Bible is what it claims to be?

We can hardly look for the kind of proof that comes from a test tube or a computer printout when we're dealing with matters of salvation or eternal life. What kind of experiment could we set up that would answer this question? Where do we look for evidence?

External Evidence

Certainly there are nonbiblical witnesses as to the truth of Scripture. Archaeology, for instance, confirms the basic outlines of biblical history. Under the entry "Hittite," to give you one example, the 1860 edition of *Encyclopaedia Britannica* had only a few lines. It says that they were a legendary people mentioned only in the Bible.

Once the Rosetta Stone was discovered, however, scholars learned how to read Egyptian hieroglyphics. This opened up a whole new world of documents for them to read and study—documents that repeatedly mentioned the Hittites!

Today, if you look at the *Encyclopaedia Britannica*, you'll find a couple of big columns devoted to this "legendary people of the Bible," as well as 27 references to them in other articles.[2] Archaeology has proven, in other words, that the Hittites existed—just as the Bible said they did!

This doesn't mean, of course, that archaeologists have answered all the objections people

Your word is a lamp to my feet and a light for my path (Psalm 119:105, NIV).

have raised about biblical history. Far from it. Many specific questions remain. But the basic contours of the Bible story are confirmed by the findings of archaeology.

Still more evidence of the Bible's reliability comes from its fulfilled prophecies. Jesus, for example, told His disciples about the destruction of Jerusalem many years before it occurred (see Mark 13; Matthew 24; Luke 21). This and many other predictions give us yet another reason that believers through the ages have trusted the Scriptures.

Yet external matters, such as archaeology and prophecy, cannot really prove biblical claims as true. The Bible, after all, claims to be more than accurate history. It claims to do more than predict the future. *The Bible claims to be able to make us wise for salvation.* How could we ever prove such a claim?

Personal Evidence

They say that the proof of the pudding is in the eating. For the Bible, the proof must be in experience. Human lives are the only experiment that can actually test the claims of Scripture.

There are two ways this test can work. One is to see the effects of the Bible's message in the lives of others. As a teacher, for instance, I often talk to my classes about the reasons that I trust God's Word. But often, when I put my reasons for this faith on the chalkboard, the best reasons are on the other side of the lectern.

My students can testify to the trustworthiness of God's Word. I think of one, for instance, who was a rock musician and addicted to drugs. After hearing the message of Scripture and letting it point him to Jesus, he came to college and earned straight A's. He is now a minister.

I think of another student who was literally a drunk in

the gutter. One night he staggered into a meeting where the Word of God was being preached. He heard that Word, and it gave him a new vision for his life. It put him in touch with a new source of power—a source that he'd not known before. He, too, came to college, and he now pastors a large church. Students such as he confirm that the Bible is what it claims to be.

While the experience of others may be enough to arouse our interest, however, only personal experience can really convince us of Scripture's truth. Only as we come to the Bible, understand its message, and take it into our hearts—only as we do this—can we find out if it is true. Only then can we know if there is really a God of grace to whom the Bible points. Only then can we know if this God can give meaning and hope and confidence to our lives. The ultimate proof that the Bible is what it claims to be, you see, can never come secondhand.

That's why you must try this experiment yourself. Read Scripture for yourself—read the story of Jesus in Mark, for instance. Pray that God will speak to you. Meditate and listen while you read. Ask God to make you wise for salvation.

Then and only then will you find that even though every earthly authority (including my wife) is wrong at least part of the time, when it comes to the most important issues of life—meaning, purpose, salvation, destiny—you really can trust the Bible and the God who stands behind it.

There are some questions, however, that I hear every now and then about the Bible. Some who are attracted to the message of Scripture wonder about how

Still more evidence of the Bible's reliability comes from its fulfilled prophecies.

the Bible made its way from ancient times to the present, and why there are so many translations. Let's conclude this chapter by looking at three common questions about God's Word that concern some people.

What about all the translations that are on the market? How can you trust Scripture when it comes in so many different versions?

The Bible, of course, was not written in English. The Old Testament was written in Hebrew (except for a little bit in Daniel and Ezra that was written in Aramaic). The New Testament was written in Greek.

Now, a diversity of translations would be a problem if each translation were made from another translation, so that every translation got one step further away from the original.

A diversity of translations is no problem, however, if each translation goes back to the original Hebrew and Greek *and* if each translation is faithful to the original.

Fortunately, the latter is true with *almost* all the translations that we have today. There are a couple of exceptions, but almost all our translations go back to the original language and are quite accurate.

Actually, the diversity of translations is a blessing rather than a problem. Suppose, for instance, that 15 different people were to translate a Spanish newspaper into English. And let's assume that each one was talented and accurate in his or her translation. They would, of course, differ in wording, and yet they could all be trustworthy. And since one never fully captures one language

> **When it comes to the most important issues of life—meaning, purpose, salvation, destiny—you really can trust the Bible and the God who stands behind it.**

into another, having more than one translation would probably help you understand the original Spanish newspaper better.

That's how it is with the different translations of the Bible that we have today. It is a blessing that we have various translations so that we can compare and come to a better understanding of the original word.

It's been hundreds and hundreds, even thousands of years, since parts of the Scripture were written. How do we know that what the prophets and apostles really wrote way back then is what we read today?

Well, it's certainly true that we don't have any of the original manuscripts that were actually written by Isaiah or Paul or John. In fact, back in 1611 (when the King James Version was translated), most of the manuscripts upon which it was based were only a few hundred years older than the King James Version itself! At that time there was almost a 1,000-year gap between the actual writing of Scripture and the oldest existing copies. This led many scoffers to question whether there was any resemblance between what Christians read and what was actually written so long before.

Again, however, archaeology has come to the rescue. Now we have copies of significant portions of the Old Testament that date back to before the time of Christ. New Testament manuscripts have been discovered as well. We now have copies of the whole New Testament from around the year 325 and copies of whole books of the New Testament from about the year 200. There is even one tiny fragment of a manuscript from the Gospel of John that was probably written around 125 C.E., maybe just 30 years after the Gospel of John was written.

That long gap of 1,000 years has been bridged, therefore, and we have found that what we read is, with an unquestionable degree of certainty, the basic message that the writers of the Bible actually wrote.

Naturally, since manuscripts were made by humans who make mistakes, there are differences among the manuscripts, but these are amazingly minor. In fact, good modern translations point these out by placing the major differences in footnotes. You can look at those footnotes and see how little question there actually is about what the biblical writers wrote.

What about differences within the Bible itself? There are parallel passages, for instance, in which one Gospel writer may tell a story with different details than does another writer.

We should freely acknowledge that such differences do exist. But do these differences really affect the message of the Bible? Here we need to keep our focus on the claims that the Bible itself makes.

The Bible's claims have to do with its message of salvation and with the guidance it gives us in our everyday lives. Now, much of that message is a historical message, and if the basic contours of that story were not true, one could hardly trust the Bible. But the Bible's trustworthiness doesn't stand or fall on the precise details of its stories. Its trustworthiness really depends on its ability to point us to God and to His grace.

I believe, for example, that my wife is trustworthy. When I travel, I never question her faithfulness. There is one thing I do, however, whenever I come home from a trip. I always re-add the figures in the

> **The trustworthiness of Scripture does not depend on the details of stories that may differ from one book to another, but on its message.**

checkbook. It's not that my wife can't add or subtract —she always got A's in math. But somehow, having the checkbook accurate just isn't as important to her as it is to me. Now that you know that, do you still think that I can call my wife trustworthy? Of course!

Likewise, the trustworthiness of Scripture does not depend on the details of stories that may differ from one book to another, but on its message. And its message, as we have seen, can be trusted absolutely.

In fact, that brings us to the point where we should change our emphasis from the Bible to the message of the Bible. The next three chapters focus on the experience of salvation to which the Bible points. We begin by looking at a word that is often misunderstood, the word "repent." Then we will move to the question of how we get rid of guilt and how we become better people.

---

[1] Of course, when Paul wrote his letter, his "Scripture" was what contemporary Christians call the Old Testament. Only after Paul wrote did Christians recognize that his writing—as well as those of the other apostles—was also inspired by God.

[2] *The New Encyclopaedia Britannica*, 15th ed. (1981), s.v. "Hittite."

CHAPTER 3

A New Look at an Old Word

When you think of the word "repent," does your mind conjure up a picture of a street preacher such as the one I saw on a corner in a busy city recently? He had a loud voice and shouted to all who passed, "Repent! The end is near!"

It's enough to give repentance a bad name. Most of us would probably rather pass by on the other side of the street and not hear about repentance. Somehow, the whole idea doesn't seem very appealing. And yet it is often the word emphasized first when we think about salvation. Many preachers tell us that the Bible message begins by calling on us to repent.

It is true that the Bible talks about repentance. But the picture it gives is quite different from the one so popularly presented.

What is repentance? How does one repent? What difference does it make to repent? What does the Bible have to say about these questions?

Interestingly, 17 of the 27 books of the New Testament do not even mention the noun *repentance* or the verb *repent*. We don't find these words, for instance, in the Gospel or letters of John, in James, or in 10 of Paul's letters. In fact, almost half (25 out of 56) of the occurrences of *repent* and *repentance* in the New Testament occur in the works of one author, Luke. Luke wrote both the Gospel of Luke and the book of Acts, and he is the New Testament writer who especially emphasizes repentance. Therefore, let's focus on these two books as we try to understand what the Bible says about repentance.

We will ask three questions. First, *what* is repentance? Second, *whose work* is repentance, God's or ours? And, finally, *what difference* does repentance make, anyway?

Technically, the background of the word translated "repentance" in the New Testament would suggest that the term primarily means a change of mind. However, this definition is much too simplistic to do justice to Luke's thought. Repentance is not just changing one's mind, nor is it merely a matter of being sorry (which is the way we often use the word in everyday speech). For Luke, repentance is radically redirecting the life from sin to God.

According to Luke, the very purpose of Jesus' ministry in the world was this refocusing of our lives on God. Jesus says that He came to call sinners *to repentance* (see Luke 5:32). And at the end of His ministry, Jesus' last words to His disciples include

> *We will ask three questions. First, what is repentance? Second, whose work is repentance, God's or ours? And, finally, what difference does repentance make, anyway?*

the promise that *repentance* and forgiveness of sins would be preached to all the nations (see Luke 24:47).

Too often we think that repentance is being sorry for what we've done. And there is a connection between the two, for Paul says that godly sorrow leads to repentance (see 2 Corinthians 7:10). But Luke makes it clear that repentance is something much more dynamic and action-oriented than simply feeling sorry.

Luke records that both Peter (see Acts 3:19) and Paul (see Acts 26:20) associate repentance with turning to God. To repent is to refocus one's life on God's plan and purpose. It means recognizing that we are sinners, that God has provided for our salvation in Jesus Christ, and that God, therefore, has a claim on our lives.

When Peter preaches in Acts 3 and 4, he shows that repentance means a total response of faith to the salvation that God has provided in Jesus Christ. In fact, Peter says that this is the only way that we can receive salvation. He begins his speech by calling his hearers to repent, and then he goes on to say of Jesus Christ, "Salvation is found in no one else, for there is no other name under heaven given to men by which we must be saved" (Acts 4:12). All this implies, of course, that one must first hear the good news of God's salvation provided in Jesus Christ before he or she can repent. For repentance is a response—a response to God's love in which we change our direction (our mind-set) and refocus our life in the light of the salvation and forgiveness that God has provided.

But *whose work* is this repentance? Is

> *Is repentance something we do, or is repentance something God gives? If we're going to be faithful to the Bible, we need to say yes to both.*

it something that we do? Or does God provide repentance?

On this question Luke presents us with a paradox. On the one hand, repentance is *our* action. Jesus tells His hearers that unless *they* repent, *they* will perish (see Luke 13:3-5). And in his famous speech to the philosophers of Athens, Paul says, "God *commands you* to repent" (see Acts 17:30). Well, if God commands us to do it, it certainly sounds like our work, doesn't it? Nothing could be clearer.

But then there is the other side of the picture. When Peter is hauled before the high priest and commanded to quit preaching, he responds, "We must obey God rather than men!" (Acts 5:29). Then he goes on to explain that God raised Jesus from the dead and exalted Him "that he might *give repentance* and forgiveness of sins to Israel" (Acts 5:31). Peter says that *God* gives repentance and forgiveness. Luke says the same in Acts 11:18. And Paul speaks of God giving repentance in 2 Timothy 2:25.

So which is it? Is repentance something *we* do, or is repentance something *God* gives? If we're going to be faithful to the Bible, we need to say yes to both. But that sounds contradictory, and it certainly doesn't explain what the Bible *means*.

There is no simple answer here. It is a genuine paradox. But perhaps it helps to realize that repentance would be impossible without God. Our very capacity to repent is a gift from God. Repentance, like forgiveness and salvation, is possible only because God, in and through Jesus Christ, took the initiative to reach out to us while we were sinners and offer us His grace. Therefore, repentance is a gift from God. He is the one who makes it possible for us to repent. But, on the other hand, God cannot force us to receive His gift. It requires action on our part. God gives repentance, but we must receive it by acting to turn our lives toward Him and refocus our direction.

You see, God is a God of forgiveness. Forgiveness for Him is more than an occasional act. It is the way He is. His disposition is to forgive. But we can appropriate God's forgiveness in our own lives only when we respond positively. Repentance is one of several terms that the Bible uses to describe this response.

Repentance emphasizes that our response includes a recognition of our sin, a sorrow for it, a desire for a different kind of life, and a turning to God to find that life. This turning to God includes believing His Word, trusting His promises, and committing ourselves to His values. And, as Peter makes it clear in Acts 2:38, it also involves baptism as a public declaration of our new direction and commitment. Finally, it also means a new life. But that brings us to our last question. *So what?* What difference does repentance make? Luke points to at least three results of repentance.

First, repentance brings joy in heaven. After telling a story about a lost sheep that was found and brought back to the fold by the shepherd, Jesus says, "I tell you that in the same way there will be more rejoicing in heaven over one sinner who repents than over ninety-nine righteous persons who do not need to repent" (Luke 15:7).

After a similar story about a woman who lost her coin and then found it, Jesus said, "In the same way, I tell you, there is rejoicing in the

> *God is a God of forgiveness. Forgiveness for Him is more than an occasional act. It is the way He is. His disposition is to forgive.*

presence of the angels of God over one sinner who repents" (verse 10).

Remember that Jesus' purpose was to bring us to repentance. All Heaven rejoices when that purpose is fulfilled, because God cares about each of us. Repentance brings joy in heaven.

Second, repentance brings the forgiveness of sins and the assurance of God's acceptance and salvation to every person who repents. "Repent, then, and turn to God, so that your sins may be wiped out" (Acts 3:19).

Think of it! Your sins are wiped out. No matter what you've done or how many times you have done it, no matter how guilty you may feel, no matter how unforgiving people may be toward you, when you repent, God wipes out your sins. They are no more. You stand before God with a clean slate. He doesn't wait for anything. He asks only that you repent. In other words, He asks that you redirect your life toward Him, turn away from sin, and trust His promise to save you freely by His grace.

Finally, repentance brings a difference in your life. It doesn't just have to do with abstract theology. It has to do with the way we live—our everyday behavior, our moral values, our ways of relating to other people. When you redirect your attention to Jesus Christ, He not only forgives the sins of the past, but He comes to be with you and give you the ability to live a new life. You don't have to go on living in sin.

John the Baptist, Jesus' cousin and forerunner, made that clear in his call to repentance. He told his hearers not only to repent, but to "produce fruit in keeping with [your] repentance" (Luke 3:8).

His hearers questioned him about this "fruit" of repentance and asked what they should do. His replies were very practical and down to earth.

John the Baptist said that a person with two coats should share with someone who had none, and that the person who had plenty of food should share with the hungry. When tax collectors asked what they should do, he told them to collect no more tax than was actually owed. (Tax collectors were known for lining their own pockets by collecting extra taxes.) When soldiers asked what they should do, the Baptist replied, "Don't extort money and don't accuse people falsely—be content with your pay" (see Luke 3:10-14).

In other words, repentance leads to very practical, down-to-earth results. It leads to a different lifestyle. Repentance is not only sorrow for sin. It is not only turning toward God. Repentance is also turning away from sin. As Paul says in Acts 26:20, "I preached that they should repent and turn to God and prove their repentance by their deeds." The proof of repentance is in the results.

A life genuinely appreciative of God's grace and refocused on Him is a life of love and compassion that mirrors God's values in its own moral behavior. In other words, when God asks us to repent, He promises not only the good news of forgiveness and a clean slate, but also power for change that lets us live in a different way. Not only are we sorry for what we have done in the past, but we have the hope of new life in the future. All this makes repentance doubly good news.

Recently our family went out to eat at one of our favorite restaurants. It's a popular place, and, as always, we had to wait almost an hour to get a table. While we waited, I read the various signs around the room. One that has always been displayed prominently since the establishment opened says: "We are sorry that we do not accept any checks."

34

I wonder how sorry they really are. Although the sign has been there for years, I have noticed no desire or even an inclination on their part to change their policy. Their "sorrow" appears to be nothing more than a polite but hollow expression. It has not led to the kind of repentance that the Bible talks about.

We, however, have the privilege of true repentance. This privilege is a gift of God's grace that offers us both forgiveness and the possibility of a new life.

With all this in mind maybe we need to reevaluate our image of repentance. Because of our preconceived ideas, repentance doesn't seem very appealing to most of us. But when we see what the Bible really says about it, the picture changes. True repentance is as appealing as the assurance that our sins are forgiven and as attractive as a changed life.

> *Repentance is not only sorrow for sin. It is not only turning toward God. Repentance is also turning away from sin.*

CHAPTER 4

How to Get Rid of Guilt

My wife had already gone to work that morning, and I had to make sure that the kids ate breakfast and got off to school on time, lunches in hand. My son Larry, now grown and married but a first grader at the time, usually did a good job of getting up on his own and getting ready. Busy making breakfast and lunches, I hardly noticed that he hadn't yet appeared.

"Laura! Larry!" I called into the other room. "It's time to come for breakfast." Laura came immediately, but there was no sign of Larry. I decided that he must be sleeping in, so I went to his bedroom. The bed was empty.

Maybe he's playing his favorite game of hide-and-seek, I thought. If so, I didn't have time for that. I yelled, "Come on, Larry. No time for games this morning." Still no response.

Finally, with some impatient frustration, I started looking in all the usual places. At last I opened a closet door and saw him standing behind the hanging clothes.

"OK, Larry, I found you," I told him. "Time to come out."

"I don't want to come out," he replied.

"What do you mean, you don't want to come out? It's time to go to school."

"I don't want you to see me," he said. "You're going to be mad."

I promised that I wouldn't get angry with him and asked, "Why would I be mad at you?"

"Because of the way I look."

I assured him that he looked fine, but he needed to hurry.

Again, he made me promise, "Don't be mad at me."

Finally, after several promises, he emerged from hiding. As soon as he got in the light, I could see the problem.

Back in those days Larry had a habit. Whenever he got a new toy, he took it to bed with him. No matter what it was—baseball, fire engine, or car—it always went to bed with him. The evening before, he had gotten a new toy—Silly Putty. It came inside a little plastic egg, but the plastic egg had come open during the night, and now Larry's hair was filled with Silly Putty.

Have you ever tried to get Silly Putty out of someone's hair? Probably not. I can tell you, though, that it's impossible. I ended up having to cut it out, and I'm not much of a barber. But at least Larry was able to go to school.

> *For every one of us there is a gap between what we do and what we would like to do, between what we are and what we would like to be. That gap, that difference, causes us to feel guilty and makes us want to hide.*

Until he got it out, however, he didn't want to be seen. He was ashamed of the way he looked.

Have you ever felt that way? Not necessarily because you had Silly Putty in your hair, but because you didn't want people to see you as you were? You wanted to hide. Maybe you didn't even want to see yourself in the mirror.

For every one of us there is a gap between what we do and what we would like to do, between what we are and what we would like to be. That gap, that difference, causes us to feel guilty and makes us want to hide.

And, of course, if we want to hide from others, if we don't even want to see ourselves in the mirror, we certainly don't want to look into the face of God. The gap between what we are and what we wish we were not only produces guilt, but it also produces alienation from God and from others. That's why our very first parents, Adam and Eve, hid as soon as they realized that they had sinned against God. "Then the man and his wife heard the sound of the Lord God as he was walking in the garden in the cool of the day, and they hid from the Lord God among the trees of the garden" (Genesis 3:8).

But that feeling didn't end with Adam and Eve. Paul described how guilt made him feel. Consider the following verses and see if you haven't felt exactly the way Paul describes.

"I do not understand what I do. For what I want to do I do not do, but what I hate I do. And if I do what I do not want to do, I agree that the law is good. As it is, it is no longer I myself who do it, but it is sin living in me. I know that nothing good

Trying harder won't solve our problems of guilt and alienation. In fact, Paul says that trying harder can actually make things worse.

lives in me, that is, in my sinful nature. For I have the desire to do what is good, but I cannot carry it out. For what I do is not the good I want to do; no, the evil I do not want to do—this I keep on doing. Now if I do what I do not want to do, it is no longer I who do it, but it is sin living in me that does it. So I find this law at work: When I want to do good, evil is right there with me. For in my inner being I delight in God's law; but I see another law at work in the members of my body, waging war against the law of my mind and making me a prisoner of the law of sin at work within my members. What a wretched man I am! Who will rescue me from this body of death?" (Romans 7:15-24).

We have all made resolutions and hoped that we could do better, only to find ourselves falling again. How do we solve this problem?

You can find any number of proposed solutions today, but I believe that they all fall under two major categories—the method of achievement or the method of acceptance.

The method of achievement is illustrated by a televised interview I saw. The reporter asked an Olympic diver why he devoted so much of his life and energy to diving. The athlete replied, "I feel that there has to be some area of life in which I am better than anyone else in the world."

Many of us feel the same way. We feel that we must achieve more than others in order to find meaning and an identity for our lives. And to find freedom from guilt.

But in the spiritual realm, the method of achievement doesn't work. Trying harder won't solve our problems of guilt and alienation. In fact, Paul says that trying harder can actually make things worse. In Romans 7:7-12 Paul says that he wouldn't have known what it was to covet except that the law said he should not covet. And then when he tried to obey the law, he seemed to covet all the more. He makes it clear that he doesn't blame the law. The law is holy and just and good. But his own nature is such that the harder he tries to obey the law, the more difficult it is for him.

Maybe an illustration will help us understand what Paul is saying. For years I often played a game with my son. I would walk up to him and say, "Larry, I'm going to count to 10, and I don't want you to laugh until I get to 10." Immediately he would become very solemn with a resolute frown on his face. I would start counting, but by the time I got to two the frown was becoming a grin. By three or four, his hands were over his mouth, and by five he was usually rolling on the floor in laughter.

Now, normally he had no trouble going for 10 seconds in life without laughing. But somehow when Larry focused on my command and tried not to laugh, there was no way he could keep from it.

In the spiritual world, the method of achievement works in much the same way. The harder we try on our own to obey, the worse we do. But thank God there is a second method. The method of acceptance.

The method of acceptance seems shocking to some and absurd to others. It claims that the very foundation of meaning and identity in life as well as our hope for the future comes in recognizing that God accepts us *just as we are*. He embraces us with His love to forgive us and make us His own without first demanding any achievement on our part. It seems too

> **According to Paul, we find meaning for the present and hope for the future only when we realize the love that God has for us.**

incredible to be true, but over and over again the Bible proclaims this as the central truth of the gospel.

After Paul sets forth his poignant expression of guilt and alienation in Romans 7, he begins Romans 8 with the good news that there is no condemnation if we are in Christ Jesus. He goes on throughout this chapter to show that we can find salvation, meaning, and hope in God's promises apart from our achievement. Paul ties this good news to a specific event in history. This accepting grace, by which God reaches out to embrace us with His love and to give us meaning in life, is made possible for us and visible to us through the cross of Jesus Christ.

As Paul says in Romans 5:6-10: "You see, at just the right time, when we were still powerless, Christ died for the ungodly. Very rarely will anyone die for a righteous man, though for a good man someone might possibly dare to die. But God demonstrates his own love for us in this: While we were still sinners, Christ died for us. Since we have now been justified by his blood, how much more shall we be saved from God's wrath through him! For if, when we were God's enemies, we were reconciled to him through the death of his Son, how much more, having been reconciled, shall we be saved through his life!"

According to Paul, we find meaning for the present and hope for the future only when we realize the love that God has for us. And this love is revealed in God's willingness to send His own Son to die for us. It means that He Himself has accomplished what we could not do. Therefore, our achievement can never serve as the basis for our salvation. Only God's gracious acceptance can do that.

I can hear some

> *God has given us eternal life, and this life is in his Son (1 John 5:11, NIV).*

people say, "You have made it far too easy. What about *our* part? What about the need for moral responsibility? Don't we need to *do* something?"

I will attempt to answer these questions in the next chapter. But you will never be able to understand part two unless you have grasped the incredible good news of part one. God accepts us, apart from our achievement, and embraces us with His love. That is the only answer to our problem of guilt and alienation. That is the only way to bridge the gap between what we are and what we wish we were, what we do and what we wish we did. The answer lies not in our accomplishments, but in understanding who we really are—children of the God of the universe, who loves us and accepts us as we are.

It was Christmastime, and my wife was in charge of the church Christmas play. There was the usual Nativity scene with Mary and Joseph, the Baby, shepherds, and Wise Men. Above the shepherds, a light was to come on at a certain point in the program, showing the angels announcing Jesus' birth.

Our son was just a little guy at the time, but he volunteered to flip on the light for his mother's program. The switch was in the back of the church behind the pulpit area and couldn't be seen from the sanctuary. A speaker above it, however, would let

But he was pierced for our transgressions, he has crushed for our iniquities; the punishment that brought us peace was upon him, and by his wounds we are healed. We all, like sheep, have gone astray, each of us has turned to his own way; and the Lord has laid on him the iniquity of us all (Isaiah 53:5, 6, NIV).

42

him hear what was going on. He had to listen for just the right words that would serve as his cue to turn on the lights. He and his mother practiced several times.

When program time came, he was in place, ready to listen for the right words. His mother went out in the sanctuary to begin the program. No one noticed that the speaker was turned off, and it was much too high for him to reach. He couldn't listen for the cue! It was too late to tell anyone. His mother was already on the platform. The program had started.

He wanted so badly to do it just right, but he didn't know what to do. He got more and more frustrated and finally just panicked. He flipped the switch and ran out the back door of the church to the car, where he hid and cried.

Out in the sanctuary, none of us knew that anything was wrong. Believe it or not, he had flipped the switch at exactly the right moment! When the program ended, my wife began looking for Larry to thank him for doing a good job, but she couldn't find him. We looked together, and finally found him sobbing in the car.

It took us awhile to discover the problem, but finally he let it out. He had failed. He had ruined the whole play. And you know, we had a hard time convincing him that it wasn't true. We tried to tell

God is our heavenly parent, and He is trying to get the good news through to us. We have made mistakes. There is a big gap between what we are and what we wish we were. But the good news is that He is willing to forgive us. He accepts us as we are. He embraces us with His love and invites us to be His children.

him, but he was so sure that he had failed, so sure that he had blown everything, that he just couldn't believe it. Finally, the good news got through, and the sobs changed to smiles.

God is our heavenly parent, and He is trying to get the good news through to us. We have made mistakes. There is a big gap between what we are and what we wish we were. We haven't turned on the light when we should have. But the good news is that He is willing to forgive us. He accepts us as we are. He embraces us with His love and invites us to be His children. That good news makes all the difference in life.

But once we believe and accept the good news, where do we go from there? That's the subject of our next chapter.

> **The Spirit himself testifies with our spirit that we are God's children (Romans 8:16, NIV).**

CHAPTER 5

Can I Be a Better Person?

Just after swimming to an Olympic gold medal in the 100-meter freestyle event in Los Angeles in 1984, American athlete Rowdy Gaines faced a TV reporter who wanted to know what he had to say after his victory. This usually outgoing athlete stuttered and stammered into the camera and finally said, "I don't know what to say. I had a speech all planned, but I was sure I was going to lose. I was going to say it had been a good career anyway, and it was a thrill just being here at the Olympics. I didn't expect to win. Now I'm speechless."

I have a feeling there is a good bit of Rowdy Gaines in most of us. We are unsure of ourselves. We recognize our inadequacies, and all too often we are sure that we are going to lose. Spiritually, many of us try and try and try and fail and fail and fail, until we finally decide that there is no hope.

In the previous chapter we talked about two methods of answering this dilemma—the method of achievement and the method of acceptance. We also saw that the biblical answer is the method of acceptance, the good news of God's grace. We cannot earn God's favor, but He takes the initiative to accept us and embrace us with His love.

But what then? Where do we go from there? Even when I understand that God accepts me, am I not the same person, with the same weaknesses and the same problems that I had before? How does understanding God's acceptance really make a difference?

We can answer this question in at least three ways.

The first answer says it doesn't matter what you do. You have been accepted by God, so don't worry about your actions—just do as you please. A rhyme parodies this answer by saying,

> "Free from the law,
> O happy condition,
> I can sin as I please
> And still have remission."

But this answer has some problems. First, it fails to appreciate the costliness of grace. When God chose to accept us and love us in spite of our weaknesses, it was not a flippant decision. "God so loved the world that he *gave* his one and only Son" (John 3:16). We can never look at the cross and forget that sin has awful consequences.

In fact, Paul explicitly rejects this first answer to the question How do I live after I realize that God has accepted me? Even in Paul's day there were some who liked this first answer. They

The method of acceptance realizes that God's grace, not the law, is God's answer to the problem of human sin and guilt, but it is not in any way opposed to God's law. The law shows us God's will.

said, "If God is a God of grace, then it doesn't matter what you do."

But Paul didn't agree: "What shall we say, then? Shall we go on sinning so that grace may increase? By no means! We died to sin; how can we live in it any longer?" (Romans 6:1, 2).

Later in the same chapter, he adds, "What then? Shall we sin because we are not under law but under grace? By no means! Don't you know that when you offer yourselves to someone to obey him as slaves, you are slaves to the one whom you obey—whether you are slaves to sin, which leads to death, or to obedience, which leads to righteousness?" (verses 15, 16). And earlier Paul asks the question Do we make void the law through faith? His answer is, "Not at all! Rather, we uphold the law" (Romans 3:31).

The method of acceptance realizes that God's grace, not the law, is God's answer to the problem of human sin and guilt, but it is not in any way opposed to God's law. The law shows us God's will. And the cross shows us that the violation of God's will is destructive to us and to others. We can never answer the question "How should we live after realizing that God accepts us as we are?" by saying it really doesn't matter.

Some give a second answer to the question. Some say, "Once you realize that you are forgiven, once you understand that God accepts you, you are right back where you began. God's acceptance takes care of the past, but now you must get on the ball and maintain that acceptance by your good works."

This answer

But grow in the grace and knowledge of our Lord and Savior Jesus Christ (2 Peter 3:18, NIV).

makes the gospel a good news/bad news joke. The good news is that you have been saved, forgiven, and accepted. The bad news is that if you don't get on the stick and achieve, you will now be rejected.

But Paul rejects this answer, too. He wrote a letter to some Christians at Galatia who believed that they must depend upon the law and their own works of salvation now that they had accepted the gospel message. Here is what he told them: "You foolish Galatians! Who has bewitched you? Before your very eyes Jesus Christ was clearly portrayed as crucified. I would like to learn just one thing from you: Did you receive the Spirit by observing the law, or by believing what you heard? Are you so foolish? After beginning with the Spirit, are you now trying to attain your goal by human effort?" (Galatians 3:1-3).

Paul rejects any answer that puts ourselves and our effort at the center of continuing Christian growth. Not only do we look to God for initial acceptance, but we look to Him for the future as well. "I thank my God every time I remember you. In all my prayers for all of you, I always pray with joy because of your partnership in the gospel from the first day until now, being confident of this, that he who began a good work in you will carry it on to completion until the day of Christ Jesus" (Philippians 1:3-6).

This brings us to the third answer. It is that we continue trusting God for growth, just as we trusted Him for acceptance. God is a God not only of grace but of growth. Paul makes this clear in Ephesians 2:8-10, "It is by grace you have been saved, through faith—and this not from yourselves, it is the gift of God—not by works, so that no one can boast. For we are God's workmanship, created in Christ Jesus to do good works, which God prepared in advance for us to do."

Notice that it is God who gives growth. God *does* expect good works from us. He *does* want us to live a life in harmony with His will, but we receive this growth by focusing on His grace and trusting Him, not by trying as hard as we can.

Have you ever decided that you were going to try to make yourself grow an inch taller? For years—through most of elementary school—my son was the shortest boy in his class, and it grated on him. Larry wanted to grow so badly that he would have done just about anything if it would have made him grow taller. But there wasn't a thing he could do except to continue to nourish himself and be patient.

Then, all of a sudden, when he turned 15, he started shooting up. Slacks that we bought a month earlier didn't fit anymore. He had to get a job after school to help pay for all those new clothes! He soon passed his mother and his sister, and now he and I look at each other eye to eye.

But my son couldn't grow just by trying harder. There certainly were things that he could have done, however, to stunt his growth. Had he never received the proper nourishment, that growth spurt would never have come. And the same is true spiritually. We can nourish our spiritual lives by coming to know Jesus better through reading His Word, talking with Him in prayer, and

> *God does expect good works from us. He does want us to live a life in harmony with His will, but we receive this growth by focusing on His grace and trusting Him, not by trying as hard as we can.*

keeping our eyes focused on His values and character. When we put our trust in Him, growth will come. It may not be as fast as we wish. We may find ourselves making mistakes that we don't really want to make. We may need to have a lot of patience. But if our focus is on Him rather than on self, growth will come. We have to trust God not only for grace and acceptance but for growth and new life, as well.

Here are two very important things to keep in mind as you think of this growth in grace. First, recognize that you will make mistakes. But don't dwell on these mistakes. Rather, trust Christ for forgiveness. Believe what John tells us: "My dear children, I write this to you so that you will not sin. But if anybody does sin, we have one who speaks to the Father in our defense—Jesus Christ, the Righteous One" (1 John 2:1).

Second, always keep your eyes focused on the right place—on Jesus Christ, who gives the growth. "Those who live according to the sinful nature have their minds set on what that nature desires; but those who live in accordance with the Spirit have their minds set on what the Spirit desires. The mind of sinful man is death, but the mind controlled by the Spirit is life and peace; the sinful mind is hostile to God. It does not submit to God's law, nor can it do so. Those controlled by the sinful nature cannot please God" (Romans 8:5-8).

Although our achievement can never save us, we do have the responsibility to keep our mind focused on the right place. We're surrounded by all kinds of pictures and images in the media

> *Although our achievement can never save us, we do have the responsibility to keep our mind focused on the right place.*

that are opposed to the mind of Christ. Illicit sex, violence, and evil will detract the mind from Christ, stunt our growth, and keep us from receiving the nourishment that we need for growth. Our work is not to earn our salvation by our own achievement but to keep our eyes focused on the source of spiritual nourishment and growth.

We have seen that God accepts us. What difference does that make?

If we grasp the enormity of His grace, it will certainly give us the desire to live a life that is worthy of His grace. And we can live that life if we put our trust in Him and depend upon Him for growth.

One early spring day I decided to go all by myself—except for taking along a pair of binoculars and a bird book—to a wildlife sanctuary so that I could enjoy the out-of-doors. It rained and was cold, but I found a shelter from the rain and enjoyed myself immensely as I watched the wildlife on a beautiful lake. Because it was so cold and rainy, I was the only person there. I finally decided that I, too, should go home and started driving the five-mile-long road that looped back to the highway.

I must have been too engrossed with the scenery, because I ended up at the side of the dirt road in a mud puddle. I tried to back the car up, but the wheels just spun in the mud. I tried to move forward, and they spun a little deeper. I tried to rock back and forth, and they went deeper yet. Finally, I got out of the car. There was no way I was going to drive out of there without doing some digging. I tried to find twigs and rocks to make a ramp.

The more I tried to get the car out, the deeper I got.

It was not only embarrassing but a little scary to be out there by myself with my car stuck in the mud. But soon things got even more embarrassing. As I got down under the car to dig, I caught my pants and ripped out the seat. Now not only was I stuck in the mud, but my pants were ripped. I had no choice but to start walking toward a ranger station two miles away. I locked the car (my binoculars were inside) and started walking. When I shoved my hand into my pocket, it seemed strangely empty. Something ought to be there. My car keys! I had locked them inside my car. I went back to see if perhaps in my absentmindedness I had forgotten to lock one of the doors. But I had done a good job, and they were all locked.

My car was stuck in the mud, my keys were locked in the car, and the seat was ripped out of my pants. I started for the ranger station again, and just then it poured down rain. Now I was also soaked.

It took a bit of courage to walk up to the ranger station when I got there, but it was my only hope. I knocked on the door, and no one answered! I started walking the long three miles out to the highway. Soon a car came along, and I stopped it. The three persons inside looked at me strangely as I explained my whole embarrassing predicament. (There was really no way to hide it.) But they were very kind and drove me to my car. We were able to push the car out of the mud, and they even had an implement that we could insert inside the window and unlock the door. Before long I was on the road again and headed for home.

I can assure you that I drove carefully. I didn't want to get stuck in the mud again. Can you imagine what those kind people would have thought if I had said, "Thank you so much for getting me out of the mud. I really appreciate it. But I can't wait to get stuck again, now that I know someone will get me out"?

God, by His grace, has rescued us from the mud of guilt and alienation. How can we possibly respond by thanking Him and then getting back into the mud? Let's keep our eyes fixed on Him, so that He can lead us safely through this life to a new and better life with Him.

In chapters 3, 4, and 5 we have focused on the present experience of salvation, as we overcome guilt and alienation from God and enter into a new experience with Him. But what about the future? We need salvation not only from guilt and alienation but also from death. What is it that God has in store for us and our world?

In the next several chapters we will take a look at the way God has solved the dilemmas of death and the future as well.

> *Do not conform any longer to the pattern of this world, but be transformed by the renewing of your mind. Then you will be able to test and approve what God's will is—his good, pleasing and perfect will (Romans 12:2, NIV).*

CHAPTER 6

Bang, Whimper, or What?

On the campus where I have taught for more than 20 years, we have added new buildings from time to time. It's always interesting to see them take shape and finally come to life with classrooms and labs, students and teachers. But the most spectacular event I can remember on campus was the demise of a building, a large auditorium that disappeared in a frightfully short time when an arsonist set it on fire.

It wasn't the first fire of the night in town. A young man started it all by burning a school bus. When that wasn't enough excitement for him, he burned down a garage with a brand new car in it. We heard the alarm for that fire. Our children, who were then only 9 and 11 years old, were already in bed. But since my wife and I were curious, we got them out of bed, dressed them, and went to the fire a few blocks away, just in time to see that it had been put out.

When we went back home, the children informed us that they didn't want to be awakened again unless they were going to see a real fire. In the middle of that night they certainly did see a real fire!

Our first clue was the volunteer fireman next door screeching out his driveway. Then we heard the alarm. Again, we looked out the window, and we could see smoke—this time it was clearly coming from the campus. Because of our children's instructions, we didn't leave right away. We stood on the front porch and watched. But as the smoke got higher and thicker, my wife couldn't stand the curiosity any longer. I agreed to stay with the children while she got in the car and went down to see what it was that was burning. She left in our Chevrolet while I stood there watching.

Then the smoke burst into a pillar of flames. I was afraid that it was the old administration building on campus, where all my notes and books and files were housed in my office.

I decided that if I got on my bicycle, I could go to a point down the street where I could get a clear view of the campus and still never take my eyes off the house, where the children were sleeping. As I pedaled down the street, I saw a car turn onto our street. It was coming from the direction of the fire. I could tell that it was a Chevrolet, and so I assumed that my wife was coming back. I turned the bicycle around and started pedaling back toward home.

I was right. It was a Chevrolet. But I was also wrong. It wasn't my wife. It was a policeman out looking for suspects, and here I was pedaling on a bicycle at 2:00 in the morning *away from* the fire.

He pulled me over and started asking questions. I told him the perfectly logical story that I've

The Bible says that we have a Friend who is going to come to the rescue of our world.

55

just told you, but somehow it didn't seem believable to him. When I told him that I had turned around because I thought it was my wife coming down the street, he said something like "Your wife, huh? Do I look like your wife?" I really got worried when he went over and called on his radio for reinforcements to arrest the suspect that he now had in custody.

Pretty soon another police car came up, lights flashing, screeching to a halt. The policeman jumped out of the car, and it was a friend of mine. In fact, he was one of my students. He was taking a class from me at that very time, and there was a test coming up in a few days. Needless to say, my ordeal ended quickly. It was good to have a friend come to the rescue.

The Bible says that we have a Friend who is going to come to the rescue of our world. A few decades ago many Christians believed that every day in every way the world was getting better and better. They believed that Christians by their effort would soon bring about God's kingdom right here on this earth.

But several things have happened in the twentieth century, and that kind of optimism has given way to a pessimism that asks whether the world will end with a bang or a whimper. Whether it will be a nuclear explosion or pollution that brings the world as we know it to an end.

But God's plan for our world is not a destructive explosion that destroys human life or a cloud of poisonous air that eventually chokes us all to death. God's plan is that the same

And if I go and prepare a place for you, I will come back and take you to be with me that you also may be where I am (John 14:3, NIV).

Saviour who died on the cross for us will return to restore our world and our lives to the joyful existence that He originally intended.

Let's turn to the Bible and ask three questions about this promise. First, *how* is Jesus going to return? Second, *when* will He return? And finally, *why* is He going to return?

How?

In Acts 1:6 we see Jesus gathered with His disciples 40 days after His resurrection. After Jesus' final instructions to them that they will receive power when the Holy Spirit comes on them and will become His witnesses in Jerusalem, all Judea, and Samaria, and to the ends of the earth, Jesus was taken up before their very eyes. A cloud took Him from their sight. And while they were still watching, two men dressed in white stood beside them and said, "Men of Galilee, why do you stand looking into heaven? This Jesus, who was taken up from you into heaven, will come in the same way as you saw him go into heaven" (Acts 1:11, RSV).

Jesus was lifted visibly from His disciples, and then they were told that He was going to return in the same way. Visibly. They would see Him come. Actually, Jesus had told the disciples the same thing earlier, shortly before His death. He warned them that there would be some who would claim that Christ had come secretly and was here or there, but Jesus warned, "So if anyone tells you, 'There he is, out in the desert,' do not go out; or, 'Here he is, in the inner rooms,' do not believe it. For as lightning that comes

Jesus will come visibly for all to see. Jesus compares it to lightning that shines clear across the sky.

from the east is visible even in the west, so will be the coming of the Son of Man" (Matthew 24:26).

Again, we learn that Jesus will come visibly for all to see. Jesus compares it to lightning that shines clear across the sky.

We get further details from the apostle Paul, who shows us some of the events to be associated with this visible return of Jesus. "For the Lord himself will come down from heaven, with a loud command, with the voice of the archangel and with the trumpet call of God, and the dead in Christ will rise first" (1 Thessalonians 4:16).

These encouraging words tell us that Jesus is going to return again. That His return will be visible. That there will be a call of the archangel, a trumpet sound, and that at that time those who have died in Christ will be brought to life. Then we who are alive will be caught up together with them, and all will go to live with Christ forever. We'll focus in more detail on this wonderful promise of the resurrection in a later chapter, but now let's move to the second question, When?

When?

The first thing we need to notice about this question is that we don't know the answer. Jesus makes that clear in Matthew 24:36, where He says, "No one knows about that day or hour, not even the angels in heaven, nor the Son, but only the Father." Now that's hard for human beings to accept. We're a curious and an impatient lot. We see that especially in children, but I have a feeling that what we see on the surface in them is really just a little deeper in all of us.

We don't know when He will come. However, He has left us signs to help and encourage us while we wait.

58

I remember when our children were very small, ages 3 and 5. We had just moved to the Pacific Northwest from southern California. All our relatives were still in California, and on the first Christmas we decided to go back and be with them. It was a long trip, and we were a little short of money for motels, so we decided to do it all in one day—1,129 miles.

We got up at 2:30 in the morning, and at their age the children found that exciting. It was special to get up while it was still dark to go see Grandpa and Grandma for Christmas. By 3:00 they were all dressed and ready, and we were in the car and on our way.

Seven miles down the road—in Milton-Freewater, Oregon—for the first time they said, "Are we almost there?" We tried to explain that we were going to drive while it was dark, and then it would get light and we would drive the whole day long, and then it would get dark again and we would drive some more, and finally we'd be at Grandpa and Grandma's. We were only about three or four miles down the road when we heard it again, "Are we almost to Grandpa's and Grandma's now?" I don't know how many times that day we heard the question.

Many people show the same kind of impatience when it comes to the promise that Jesus is going to return. And so they get out charts and try to figure out all kinds of mathematical calculations, but we don't know when He will come. However, He has left us signs to help and encourage us while we wait. In the next chapter we'll try to discover what these signs are all about. But now to our final question.

Why?

It is with this question that more people are misled than with any of the others. So many people find that the return of Jesus is somehow a frightening idea. The end of the world is associated with catastrophes and all kinds of scary events. While it is true that the Lord has shown us that the world will have problems before He returns, the focus in the New Testament is not on the catastrophes that happen first, but on the Person who has promised to return. Christ is coming because He cares about His people, because He loves them and wants them to be free of suffering and death. He wants them to enjoy face-to-face fellowship with Him forever.

I suppose that's one of the reasons that the promise of Jesus' second coming is compared to a wedding. Revelation 19 calls it the wedding of the Lamb and says, "Blessed are those who are invited to the wedding supper of the Lamb!" (verse 9). In fact, verse 7 commands us to rejoice and exult, for the marriage of the Lamb has come. I suspect that God compares the return of Jesus with a wedding because He wants us to have the same sense of excitement and joy that young lovers have as they make their vows and begin a new home together.

A few months ago I had the privilege of performing my son's wedding. It was a delight to see the excitement that he and his bride showed with each decision about their wedding and with every item that they purchased for their new home together.

Christ wants us to be together in a new home with Him. The Second Coming ushers in this new home. It leads to a new heaven and a new earth. See if you can't sense that same excitement as you meditate on what the book of Revelation tells us about this

> *Christ wants us to be together in a new home with Him. The Second Coming ushers in this new home.*

new heaven and earth.

"Then I saw a new heaven and a new earth, for the first heaven and the first earth had passed away, and there was no longer any sea. I saw the Holy City, the new Jerusalem, coming down out of heaven from God, prepared as a bride beautifully dressed for her husband. And I heard a loud voice from the throne saying, 'Now the dwelling of God is with men, and he will live with them. They will be his people, and God himself will be with them and be their God. He will wipe every tear from their eyes. There will be no more death or mourning or crying or pain, for the old order of things has passed away.' He who was seated on the throne said, 'I am making everything new!' " (Revelation 21:1-5).

Are there any signs to let us know if we are getting close to the fulfillment of this promise? We turn to that question in the next chapter.

> *And he will send his angels with a loud trumpet call, and they will gather his elect from the four winds, from one end of the heavens to the other (Matthew 24:31, NIV).*

CHAPTER 7

Interpreting the Signs

I don't remember the first time I went to church, but my folks will probably never forget it! I was only 2 weeks old at the time. I slept through the service, and when it was over, a crowd of friends gathered around my mom and dad to congratulate them and to see the new baby. The comments were typical, ranging from "He looks just like you" to "I'm so happy for you." But two women waited at the edge of the crowd until the well-wishers had left. Their comments were different! They had something else in mind altogether.

They approached my parents and said, "We wish we could congratulate you on the birth of this child. But we cannot. We think it's a terrible thing that you have done—bringing a child into the world when Armageddon is already upon us." And then they quoted Matthew 24:19 to my parents: "Woe to those who are pregnant and to those who are nursing infants in those days!" (NRSV).

It was the middle of World War II, and these women had read their Bibles. They were watching the signs. They knew about wars and rumors of wars. It was truly a time of trouble such as the world had never seen. And it all pointed in one direction, and one direction only—the end was near. Jesus was about to come. And people like my parents, who went right on with their ordinary living, were soon to be in deep trouble. They would soon be trying to flee to the mountains with nursing babies in their arms. The words of Jesus made it clear.

Of course, my parents didn't have to flee to the mountains while I was a baby. The years have gone on, and a few weeks ago I performed *my* son's wedding. Obviously these women were mistaken. Jesus didn't come during World War II. But they weren't just mistaken about the time of the Second Coming. They were mistaken in the way they read what Matthew 24 says about the signs of the end and in the way they understood Jesus.

Before we're too hard on them, however, we need to remember that Jesus' own disciples continually misunderstood Him in very much the same way. These women and Jesus' disciples had in common the mistaken idea that when Jesus talked about signs, He was trying to let them know the time of His return. They thought that He was trying to answer the "when" question about the Second Coming.

That shouldn't be all that surprising. After all, at the beginning of Matthew 24 that is precisely what the disciples had asked about. They queried, "Tell us, *when* will this be, and what will be the sign of your coming and of the end of the age?" (Matthew 24:3, NRSV). Jesus went on to give them signs, and ever since there have been Christians who have tried to use

Jesus tried to make it clear that He simply wasn't answering the "when" question, even though that was the question they had asked.

these signs as a basis for calculation—as data to be figured so that they can answer the "when" question.

But a closer look at Matthew 24 shows that Jesus didn't try to answer the "when" question for them. Instead, He began on their ground with their question but then went on to redirect their focus.

It is true that He listed the traditional signs of the end that they would have already known from their Jewish faith. Wars and rumors of wars. Famines and pestilence. Earthquakes. But then He said, "This is just the beginning. The end is not yet!" (see verse 6).

And even after listing further signs throughout the chapter, including the darkening of the sun and the falling of the stars, and even after proclaiming that when they would see these things they would know it was near, even at the door (see verse 33), Jesus again took the focus off the "when" question by saying, in verse 36: "But about that day and hour no one knows, neither the angels of heaven, nor the Son, but only the Father" (NRSV).

Jesus tried to make it clear that He simply wasn't answering the "when" question, even though that was the question they had asked. True, He gave them specific warning about the coming destruction of Jerusalem. But concerning the Second Coming He gave them no formulas for calculating the time. That wasn't His purpose.

So what was He trying to do? Why these signs if they don't help us figure out when Christ will return? If we study the rest of Matthew 24 and 25 carefully, it is clear that *Jesus tries to direct them from the task of calculating when He will return*

Signs should remind Christians of the seriousness of Christ's kingdom and encourage them that Christ has not forgotten them.

to the task of living lives of hope and responsibility in preparation for His return.

This is evident from the flow of His discourse, which begins with the signs, but then moves to four stories that help put the signs into perspective. The signs show the kinds of events that will happen in the world while the disciples are waiting for Christ's return. Signs should remind Christians of the seriousness of Christ's kingdom and encourage them that Christ has not forgotten them. But they also must be prepared to live lives focused on the kingdom even when its final manifestation seems longer in coming than they thought. In the stories at the end of the discourse (Matthew 24:45-25:46) Jesus both prepares them for the possibility of delay and points to their continuing task.

He tells a story of a master who leaves and puts his servants in charge. In it He talks about the folly of servants who live irresponsibly and fail to carry out the master's will because they think the master is delayed. Jesus tells another story about 10 young women who are waiting for a wedding. When the bridegroom is delayed, it is the ones who are prepared with extra oil for their lamps who participate. His stories of the talents and of the sheep and the goats point to the kind of responsibility that should characterize the lives of His disciples. They will devote themselves to using the gifts He gives responsibly and especially to caring for those in need. Even though the promise may seem slow in its fulfillment to them, their task isn't calculation. Their

> **When these things begin to take place, stand up and lift up your heads, because your redemption is drawing near (Luke 21:28, NIV).**

task is living responsibly as part of God's kingdom.

Unfortunately, Jesus' original disciples didn't fully understand this message, for even when it came time for Jesus to return to heaven after His resurrection, they still were consumed with the "when" question. They asked, "Lord, is this the time when you will restore the kingdom to Israel?" (Acts 1:6, NRSV). But in the next verse, Jesus answered, "It is not for you to know the times or periods that the Father has set by his own authority" (verse 7, NRSV). He then went on to do the same kind of thing He had done in Matthew 24 and 25. He redirected their focus to the kind of life they should live. He told them that they would receive power for witness and should tell all the world about the good news.

What does all this mean for us? Are there signs that confirm our hope that the return of Christ is near?

First of all, we should recognize that if Jesus didn't let His disciples in on how to figure out when He would return and said that He Himself didn't know, we should hardly expect some inside track for ourselves! There are no events in the daily paper that will help us calculate the time. That isn't our task. Wars and rumors of wars, earthquakes and famines, simply remind us that Jesus knew what would happen in the interim before His coming. When others are frightened and feel that the world is falling apart, our hope gives us steady ground from which to encourage them and work for their needs and make the world a better place, as Jesus has instructed us. After all, Jesus saw these things coming and warned us not to give up.

So you also must be ready, because the Son of Man will come at an hour when you do not expect him (Matthew 24:44, NIV).

On the other hand, it is also true that Jesus expects us to use our heads. He said that people ought to know that when a fig tree puts forth its leaves, summer is coming. Certainly our age has become the kind of time to which Jesus pointed as the time of His return. For instance, in Matthew 24:22 He told the disciples, "And if those days had not been cut short, no one would be saved; but for the sake of the elect, those days will be cut short" (NRSV). And in Revelation 11:18, John pictures Jesus coming to destroy those who would destroy the earth.

I'm sure that when every new weapon of war was invented throughout history, it was seen by many as a sign of the end of the world. Yet, our time really is different. For the first time in the history of the world, human beings really could destroy the earth, either with the push of a button and a big bang or with the pollution that is so often a by-product of modern technology. It is truly possible now that God would have to cut short the days, lest all human population be destroyed. In other words, it would also be the height of folly to say with the wicked servant in Jesus' story, "My lord is delayed; let's eat and drink with drunkards."

Instead, the general shape of the age in which we live as well as every sign that we read in Jesus' discourse should remind us of Jesus' promised return, not so that we can figure out when He will

If Jesus didn't let His disciples in on how to figure out when He would return and said that He Himself didn't know, we should hardly expect some inside track for ourselves! There are no events in the daily paper that will help us calculate the time.

come (we can't even if we want to), but so that we can keep our focus on the kingdom and live now the kind of responsible, caring life that characterizes that kingdom and prepares us to live in it forever.

In this chapter and the previous one, we've pictured the promise of the second coming of Jesus Christ as a joyful hope that we can look forward to. Yet, is that the whole story? Doesn't the second coming of Jesus also mean judgment, and isn't that a frightening prospect? Let's turn now to that question.

> *He who stands firm to the end will be saved (Matthew 24:13, NIV).*

CHAPTER 8

Accountable! Your Turn in the Spotlight

One day as I was walking down a busy city street, an apparently sincere Christian approached me, held out a pamphlet, and said, "Won't you please read this?" Not wanting to be rude, I took the little booklet and put it in my pocket. I didn't even think of it again until I was cleaning out my pockets. Suddenly the bright red print caught my eye.

The cover showed a picture of Jesus, a Bible, and the words (in big red letters) "THE WRATH OF GOD TO YOU." I turned to the back cover and noticed large red flames. A Bible verse was printed over them, with one word of the text many times bigger than all the rest: " 'The wicked shall be turned into HELL, and all the nations that forget God' (Psalm 9:17)." When I opened the pamphlet I read many statements about wrath, hell, and judgment.

I must confess that I didn't find all this terribly appealing. In fact, I considered it incongruous. What was this depressing talk about punishment and wrath doing with that picture of Jesus on the front? Didn't whoever put this booklet together know that Jesus reveals a God of grace and forgiveness? Why, then, all this emphasis on wrath?

As I looked more closely, however, I noticed that every word of this brochure came directly from the Bible. It wasn't just someone's crazy ideas. But the fact that it came from the Bible didn't make it any more appealing. Is this *really* the Bible's message about judgment? Is God a God of wrath, judgment, punishment, and hell?

In a way, the whole subject of judgment presents a dilemma. On the one hand, Christians affirm that God is fair and just. On the other, they also see Him as kind and loving. But these two ideas do not always fit well together. If God is a just God who demands accountability, how can any of us, who know ourselves to be frail sinners, ever have any confidence and assurance about the future? But if God doesn't demand accountability, how can we make sense out of a world in which the innocent suffer and millions of lives can be taken by a dictator's acts of genocide?

Several years ago a colleague and I were attending a convention in Los Angeles. I traveled by car and agreed to pick him up when he arrived later on the plane. When I did so, he introduced me to a man he had met on the plane. This individual was going to the same convention. We invited his new acquaintance to ride with us, and once we got in the car I realized what my

> *In a way, the whole subject of judgment presents a dilemma. On the one hand, Christians affirm that God is fair and just. On the other, they also see Him as kind and loving. But these two ideas do not always fit well together.*

colleague had not—this was a famous theologian who rode with us.

He was one of the originators of the "God is dead" movement in the 1960s. One of the primary reasons he gave for espousing the view that God is dead concerned this matter of evil in the world and accountability for it. He said that when he saw the murder of 6 million Jews, he had to conclude one of two things. Either there is no all-powerful God who rules the universe, or there is a God, and He just doesn't care. He said that he found it much more acceptable to believe that there is no God.

The Bible, however, gives a different answer. It teaches that a judgment is coming when God will bring an end to evil and suffering and when He will hold all those who have contributed to evil and suffering accountable for their actions. In fact, every human being will be held accountable. This judgment comes at the end of this world's history and determines our ultimate destiny.

Paul, in the midst of admonishing the Romans that they should quit judging one another, appeals to this final judgment when he says: "We will all stand before God's judgment seat. It is written: 'As surely as I live,' says the Lord, 'every knee will bow before me; every tongue will confess to God.' So then, each of us will give an account of himself to God" (Romans 14:10, 11).

Similarly, he told the Corinthians: "We must all appear before the judgment seat of Christ, that each one may receive what is due him for the things done while in the body, whether good or bad" (2 Corinthians 5:10).

The book of Revelation also speaks of judgment. It pictures a time just before God establishes a new heaven and new earth for all eternity when everyone stands before God's throne and is judged. Those whose names are not found among the saved are then destroyed by fire.

We read: "I saw a great white throne and him who was seated on it. Earth and sky fled from his presence, and there was no place for them. And I saw the dead, great and small, standing before the throne, and books were opened. Another book was opened, which is the book of life. The dead were judged according to what they had done as recorded in the books. The sea gave up the dead that were in it, and death and Hades gave up the dead that were in them, and each person was judged according to what he had done. Then death and Hades were thrown into the lake of fire. The lake of fire is the second death. If anyone's name was not found written in the book of life, he was thrown into the lake of fire" (Revelation 20:11-15).

Obviously the God of the universe doesn't need books to determine what people on this earth have done and are doing. Today, we would at least use a computer! But these "books" are powerful symbols of the accountability that we all must face with reference to God. God is not just an onlooker. He is holding us accountable and will judge us. In fact, the Bible pictures this judgment as beginning even before Christ returns to this world. Revelation 22:12 tells us that not only is Christ coming soon but that He is also bringing His rewards with Him. Apparently the process of reviewing each life begins before the Second Coming.

> *The Bible teaches that a judgment is coming when God will bring an end to evil and suffering and when He will hold all those who have contributed to evil and suffering accountable for their actions.*

Now all this sounds ominous. God is keeping track of our lives. He is going to demand accountability of us. And this judgment will determine our ultimate destiny—either eternity with Christ in a new heaven and new earth or destruction in a lake of fire. That certainly sounds like something that would make a stern and solemn warning appropriate. Maybe the flaming red pamphlet I received on the street was right on track. Maybe my failure to find it appealing was just my problem. Maybe there should be a lot more people on the streets to warn the world of coming judgment.

I am still not convinced, however, that this pamphlet told the whole story, even though all its contents were taken right out of the Bible. You see, the Bible also tells us some other things about the judgment that we need to know if we are to see the entire picture. In fact, I believe that the overall tone of the Bible's warning about judgment is quite different from the tone of the flaming red pamphlet.

One of the ironies we find in the Bible is that judgment can be pictured as *good news*. In fact, at several points in the book of Revelation God is actually praised for judgment! This ominous accountability is actually a cause for rejoicing! It is something to shout about!

"We give thanks to you, Lord God Almighty, the One who is and who was, because you have taken your great power and have begun to reign. The nations were angry; and your wrath has come. The time has come for judging the dead, and for rewarding your servants the prophets and your saints and those who reverence your name, both small and great—and for destroying those who destroy the earth" (Revelation 11:17, 18).

Notice that there is a reason that God's judgment,

indeed even His wrath, is a cause for rejoicing. Judgment means an end to evil and suffering. With God's judgment, oppression comes to an end. Death is no more. Those who are destroyed are those who "destroy the earth."

I imagine that when those words were first written, they seemed preposterous. How could mere human beings do something as drastic as destroy this whole big earth? But the situation is different today. We really do have it in our power to destroy the earth. But as we have already seen in chapter 6 of this book, Revelation tells us that God is not going to leave our world to self-destruct in a bang of nuclear explosion or a whimper of pollution. God is still in control. He will act as judge and require a fair and just accountability and bring about an end to suffering.

But this cosmic good news still doesn't answer one side of the dilemma with which we began. Certainly the end of pain, suffering, death, and evil is good news for the world. It is also good news for those who come out on the right side of that ominous final judgment. But is it good news for *me*?

When I think of those books and that final day of judgment and then look at my own life with its weaknesses and problems, it is pretty scary. When I realize how many times I have made resolutions only to fail miserably later, it seems almost hopeless. How could I ever stand in such a scene before such a God and come out on the right side?

Fortunately, the Bible answers this question, too. And it is here that we hear the ultimate good news of the judgment. The fact is that we do not need

> **There is a reason that God's judgment, indeed even His wrath, is a cause for rejoicing.**

to worry about the judgment. When Jesus came and lived on this earth, died on the cross, came back to life, and was exalted to the throne of God, He took away our need to worry about the judgment. Notice that most familiar passage in the Bible: "God so loved the world that he gave his one and only Son, that whoever believes in him shall not perish but have eternal life. For God did not send his Son into the world to condemn the world, but to save the world through him. Whoever believes in him is not condemned" (John 3:16-18).

When we put our trust in Jesus Christ, believe that He accepts us and forgives us, and commit our lives to Him, we no longer stand under judgment. In Christ we are free of this fear. This is what Paul calls throughout his letters being "under grace." It means standing in the atmosphere of God's acceptance without fear of judgment. In fact, listen to what Jesus Himself says: "I tell you the truth, whoever hears my word and believes him who sent me has eternal life and will not be condemned; he has crossed over from death to life" (John 5:24).

The word "condemned" in this passage could be translated "judged" as well. The idea is that the one who believes in Jesus does not face the worry of a negative decision in the judgment.

In Jesus Christ we can have the assurance that we have already passed from death to life. Indeed, eternal life has already begun for us. There is no need to fear. Judgment is not only cosmic good news; it can also be personal good news. Through Jesus, God is able to be both just and

> *God will bring to judgment both the righteous and the wicked (Ecclesiastes 3:17, NIV).*

gracious, fair and loving.

No, red flames of wrath don't even begin to tell the whole story. Only when the scene includes the open, scarred hand of gracious acceptance do we see the whole picture that God has revealed about the good news of judgment.

In the past three chapters we have been surveying the good news about Jesus' second coming. Let's turn now to see how this promise of the Second Coming speaks to the problem of death. How will God conquer death and suffering through the promise of Jesus' return?

The fact is that we do not need to worry about the judgment. When Jesus came and lived on this earth, died on the cross, came back to life, and was exalted to the throne of God, He took away our need to worry about the judgment.

CHAPTER 9

When Thoughts About Death Trouble You

Death. The very word sends a certain fright into our bones. Yet with this inevitable fear we combine a kind of fascination. Notice how many movies, plays, and television programs explore the subject of death.

Volumes are being written on death, and from these writings a new doctrine has emerged emphasizing that death is a natural part of life. We should not fear death, say these proponents of a new way of looking at death. We should accept it as the last "passage" in life, the natural culmination of our lives. Some even urge that we view death as a welcome friend. In the poetic words of the mystic Kahlil Gibran, death (he calls it ceasing to breathe) releases our breath to go unencumbered to God (*The Prophet*, p. 81).

Actually this "new" doctrine is not so new. Many of the ancient philosophers looked on death in much the same way. Epicurus, who lived from 342-270 B.C., wrote: "Become accustomed to the belief that death is nothing to us. For all good and evil consists in sensation, but death is deprivation of sensation. And therefore a right understanding that death is nothing to us makes the mortality of life enjoyable, not because it adds to it an infinite span of time, but because it takes away the craving for immortality" (*Epistle to Menoeceus*, quoted in C. K. Barrett, ed., *The New Testament Background: Selected Documents*, p. 73).

Since these ideas about death have such a long history and are being emphasized so strongly today, surely it would seem that we would trust them. But, in fact, we find serious problems with this view of death as a friend.

First, it does not square with human experience. No matter how many people try to convince us that death is just a natural part of life, death remains something "unnatural." Death is not "nothing" to us. When terrorists bomb an airplane and defenseless men, women, and children lose their lives, it is definitely not nothing to us. We cannot pass it off by saying, "Oh well, death is just a natural part of life. After all, their time had to come someday." No! We are incensed and enraged.

Second, this view of death does not square with the New Testament. There death does not appear as a friend. In fact, Paul specifically calls death an enemy. He says, "The last enemy to be destroyed is death" (1 Corinthians 15:26).

The view of death as an enemy becomes obvious in Jesus' life as well. As He faced His own death He didn't welcome it as a friend or as a natural part of life. Instead, He agonized and asked that if possible He might be spared.

Notice the poignant drama: "And he said to them, 'My soul is very sorrowful, even to death; remain here, and watch.' And going a little farther, he fell on the ground and prayed that, if it were possible, the hour might pass

78

from him. And he said, 'Abba, Father, all things are possible to thee; remove this cup from me; yet not what I will, but what thou wilt' " (Mark 14:34-36, RSV).

Does this mean that the New Testament is less hopeful and optimistic about death than either ancient philosophers or modern writers? Not at all. The New Testament is full of hope. The difference lies in the *basis* for optimism. The New Testament doesn't try to encourage optimism by playing down the trauma and terror of death. It doesn't try to put a pretty face on death. It is far too realistic for that. It recognizes that death is the enemy, but despite that, it offers comfort, assurance, and hope.

The basis for hope in the New Testament is the resurrection of Jesus Christ. True, death is an enemy, but in Jesus Christ it is a *defeated* enemy, for death was not able to hold Him in the tomb. No passage of Scripture presents this truth more forcefully than 1 Corinthians 15.

Paul set forth the death and resurrection of Jesus as a matter of great significance: "I delivered to you as of *first importance* what I also received, that Christ died for our sins in accordance with the scriptures, that he was buried, that he was raised on the third day in accordance with the scriptures" (verses 3, 4, RSV).

This is the heart of the Christian faith: Jesus died and rose again. He came forth from the tomb alive. People saw Him. Peter, James, the twelve, 500 people at

> *The basis for hope in the New Testament is the resurrection of Jesus Christ. True, death is an enemy, but in Jesus Christ it is a defeated enemy, for death was not able to hold Him in the tomb.*

once, and even Paul. Paul believed that the encounter he had on the road to Damascus was actually an appearance of the risen Lord to him (1 Corinthians 15:5-10). There was no doubt in his mind that Jesus was alive.

But for Paul, the resurrection of Jesus was by no means simply the case of a revived corpse. This was not just a body that came back to life. Jesus' resurrection was the beginning of *the* resurrection, a crucial moment in salvation's history. His resurrection was intimately and integrally related to our resurrection. In His resurrection we find our basis for hope that death, though an enemy, will not have the final word.

Paul illustrates this truth by using the symbol of the "firstfruits" (verse 20). The Jews showed their gratitude for God's blessings and their trust in Him by bringing the very first part of their harvest as an offering. These firstfruits were their assurance that the remainder of the harvest would follow. The firstfruits were only the beginning of the harvest, but the ceremony expressed trust that the remainder was on the way.

The resurrection of Jesus, says Paul, is the firstfruits of those who have fallen asleep in death. It gives Christians the same kind of hope and assurance. His resurrection is only the beginning. It assures us that we, too, can look forward to victory over death. For the same God who resurrected Jesus will also bring to life those who have died with their eyes fixed on Jesus. The two resurrections, Christ's and ours, are bound so closely together that we can be certain that we, too, shall live.

Some of the

The New Testament consistently focuses the Christian's hope on the resurrection of the dead at the second coming of Jesus Christ.

Corinthian Christians apparently doubted that those who died would really be brought to life again. They didn't think the resurrection was possible. But Paul insisted that if one really understood Jesus' resurrection, he or she would understand what it meant for Jesus' followers. Notice how strongly he ties the meaning of Christian faith to the future resurrection of the dead.

"Now if Christ is preached as raised from the dead, how can some of you say that there is no resurrection of the dead? But if there is no resurrection of the dead, then Christ has not been raised; if Christ has not been raised, then our preaching is in vain and your faith is in vain. We are even found to be misrepresenting God, because we testified of God that he raised Christ, whom he did not raise if it is true that the dead are not raised. For if the dead are not raised, then Christ has not been raised. If Christ has not been raised, your faith is futile and you are still in your sins. Then those also who are fallen asleep in Christ have perished. If for this life only we have hoped in Christ, we are of all men most to be pitied" (verses 12-19, RSV).

Paul places this great event, the bringing back to life of those who have died in Christ, at the second coming of Jesus. He gives a clear description of this in his letter to the Christians at the city of Thessalonica: "The Lord himself will descend from heaven with a cry of command, with the archangel's call, and with the sound of the trumpet of God. And the dead in Christ will rise first; then we who are alive, who are left, shall be caught up together with them in the clouds to meet the Lord in the air; and so we shall always be with the Lord. Therefore comfort one another with these words" (1 Thessalonians 4:16-18, RSV).

At Jesus' return the faithful dead are raised, and the

righteous living are caught up with them to meet the Lord. But this is not all. These resurrected ones are also changed. In this life they have been mortal, subject to the inevitable enemy, death. But at the sound of the last trumpet that hails the return of Jesus, they become immortal, and death's defeat becomes a reality (see 1 Corinthians 15:51-53).

Sense the spirit of celebration and victory in Paul's words as he proclaims the good news that death is swallowed up in victory: "When the perishable puts on the imperishable, and the mortal puts on immortality, then shall come to pass the saying that is written: 'Death is swallowed up in victory.' 'O death, where is thy victory? O death, where is thy sting?' The sting of death is sin, and the power of sin is the law. But thanks be to God, who gives us the victory through our Lord Jesus Christ" (verses 54-57, RSV).

The New Testament consistently focuses the Christian's hope on the resurrection of the dead at the second coming of Jesus Christ, not on an immediate flight to the heavenly realm at the time of death. It views death as a sleep, an unconscious waiting for the time of the resurrection. Over and over again both Jesus and Paul refer to death as sleep. It is those who are "asleep" who participate in the resurrection. What we look forward to is not an ethereal, disembodied existence, but the restoration of physical life in an earth made new. And this restored body will be a new body, no longer subject to death. Paul calls it a "spiritual" body (verse 44). By this he does not mean bodiless existence, but an immortal body that manifests the

The resurrection is God's declaration that physical life, though corrupted by sin, is redeemable.

benefits of Christ's victory over death.

Here, then, is what we have learned from the Bible about death: In the New Testament death is not a welcome friend but an enemy. Yet it is an enemy that has lost its sting. In fact, the enemy has already been defeated, for Jesus revealed God's power over death when He came forth from the tomb. But Jesus' resurrection is only the firstfruits, the guarantee, that assures our resurrection as well. At the Second Coming the dead in Christ will be resurrected to immortal life, and the living righteous will be instantaneously transformed to immortality. Thus death will be swallowed up in victory.

This biblical view has a number of significant implications not just for the future but that make a difference in our lives right now. First, it means that we can live with both realism and confidence—realism that recognizes and admits the evil of death, as well as confidence that focuses on the future promise. We no longer have to deny death's sting in order to escape its terror. Rather we rest in the assurance of Christ's victory.

Second, it means that we can affirm physical existence as good, for the promise of the resurrection shows that God affirms it. The resurrection is God's declaration that physical life, though corrupted by sin, is redeemable. Some early Christians, whose views the church decided were heretical, believed that the ultimate future hope was total escape from all things

> *God . . . alone is immortal and . . . lives in unapproachable light. . . . To him be honor and might forever. Amen (1 Timothy 6:15, 16, NIV).*

physical and material. Some of them concluded that as far as possible all physical enjoyment—such as food and sexual expression—must therefore be rejected. But Christians who accept the New Testament teaching on the resurrection will see physical life as a gift of God, to be enjoyed responsibly according to God's will as expressed in His law.

Third, it means that we do have a responsibility to the body now. Although some of these early Christians tried to escape physical things by rejecting them, others concluded that since hope for the future meant escape from physical existence, the body was ethically insignificant. One could do with the body whatever one wished—it didn't matter. They even willingly sanctioned sexual immorality, for example. In fact, even some Christians in Corinth apparently took such a view.

Paul had absolutely no sympathy for their position, however. In 1 Corinthians 6:12-20 he actually uses the resurrection as an argument for Christian moral responsibility. Our bodies belong to God. He cares enough about them to resurrect them. Therefore we should use them responsibly and glorify God in our bodies (see verse 20).

Finally, the biblical view of death and resurrection means that life is filled with new meaning and purpose. One of the greatest diseases of our time is the sense of futility and meaninglessness that so many feel. But the truth of the resurrection not only teaches us that life—present, physical life—is

Our bodies belong to God. He cares enough about them to resurrect them. Therefore we should use them responsibly and glorify God in our bodies.

good, but it also shows us that we have a marvelous destiny that goes beyond this life. We see that God has a new life for us that transcends death. Therefore we live in confident assurance, knowing that "from [heaven] we await a Savior, the Lord Jesus Christ, who will change our lowly body to be like his glorious body, by the power which enables him even to subject all things to himself" (Philippians 3:20, 21, RSV).

At this point we should explore further how this biblical teaching helps us understand not only death, but human life as well. What are human beings, anyway? Who are we? We now turn to one of the psalms in the Old Testament that helps us answer that question.

> *The living know that they will die, but the dead know nothing (Ecclesiastes 9:5, NIV).*

CHAPTER 10

Who Are We?

When we moved to a rural area away from the city lights, our family thoroughly enjoyed a new summer evening activity. We loved to put a blanket on the back lawn, lie on our backs, and just look at the sky's countless lights. What a majestic, awesome sight! Somehow the world suddenly shrinks, and we become lost in the overwhelming spectacle.

The very same sight inspired the psalmist to reflect on the place of human beings in the universe and to ask the question "What is man?" In Psalm 8 he says: "When I consider your heavens, the work of your fingers, the moon and the stars, which you have set in place, what is man that you are mindful of him, the son of man that you care for him?" (verses 3, 4).

In the light of the vastness of the heavens and the glory of the stars, we might expect a very negative answer—a human being is a tiny speck in a vast cosmic sea, small and insignificant.

But this is far from the answer of the psalmist. Even as he stood in amazement at the moon and stars, he responded: "You made him a little lower than the heavenly beings and crowned him with glory and honor. You made him ruler over the works of your hands; you put everything under his feet: all flocks and herds, and the beasts of the field, the birds of the air, and the fish of the sea, all that swim the paths of the seas. O Lord, our Lord, how majestic is your name in all the earth!" (verses 5-9).

According to the psalmist, God created humans only a little lower than God Himself, and He crowned them with glory and honor, and gave them dominion over everything in this world.

Well, all of that sounds very nice. In fact, it is beautiful poetry. But is it believable? Hasn't the psalmist gotten a little carried away? (After all, poets often do.) What I mean is this: Do *you* feel like you have dominion over everything? Or do you feel dominated by all kinds of forces beyond your control—from recession to big government to the boss? Do you *really* feel just a little lower than God, or do you struggle some days just to feel human?

Was the psalmist wrong? How can the psalmist say such things? Obviously he had never seen Auschwitz or Vietnam. He had never struggled to make ends meet on a limited budget or watched the prices soar at the gas pump and the supermarket. And, of course, he didn't have access to modern scientific data that many claim reveals humans as nothing more than a

> *According to the psalmist, God created humans only a little lower than God Himself, and He crowned them with glory and honor, and gave them dominion over everything in this world.*

species of hairless bipeds that has evolved the intelligence to use complicated tools and abstract language.

But before we pass the psalmist off too quickly, perhaps we should try to understand what he said in the light of the rest of the Scriptures. In fact, if we are really to understand him, we must go two directions. First, we must go back to Genesis, for the psalmist grounded these seemingly unbelievable assertions in the affirmation that God is Creator. Second, we must go forward to the New Testament, for New Testament writers used this psalm in a way that not only helps explain its meaning but also helps answer our basic question, Who are we?

The psalmist's optimistic picture of the human race rests soundly on a concept of Creation. God made us humans a little lower than Himself. All that we are, we owe to God. He created us in His own image to rule the earth and enjoy it. When we read the first two chapters of the Bible, we see ourselves as children of God.

But the biblical Creation account also gives other quite specific information about who humans are. It shows that God created humans both male and female. In fact, it is as male and female that they bear the image of God.

Genesis 2:7 shows yet another aspect of who humans are. God formed the first humans from the dust of the earth and breathed life into them. Then the first human became a living soul, or person. Many believe that the *real* person is a soul that lives within the body. But here we see that the soul—body plus breath—is the total, unified person. Souls are not entities that

> **All that we are, we owe to God. He created us in His own image to rule the earth and enjoy it.**

live within humans. Rather, human beings are souls in their total person. The Bible always pictures the human as a unity. The body is not just a shell for the soul, but a part of the unified, indivisible person.

There is yet something else we find out about humans in the Creation story. Genesis 3 tells us that humans have fallen. They failed to achieve the plan for which God created them. As a result, the first humans suffered, the earth suffered, and humans continue to suffer.

But the Fall isn't the end of the story. Remember, we said that to understand the psalmist we needed to go back to Creation *and* forward to the New Testament.

In Ephesians 1 we hear the good news that there is one Man to whom this psalm does apply. Even though all those glowing things don't seem to fit us, they do fit Someone. Jesus Christ came to this earth as a human being. In fact, He was *the* human being, a new Adam. But He didn't fall. Through His perfect life, death, and resurrection, He gained the victory. Now the words of Psalm 8, those glowing words that sound so unrealistic to us, do apply to Him.

Notice how the words of Psalm 8 appear in this description of Jesus in Ephesians 1:20-23: ". . . which he [God] exerted in Christ when he raised him from the dead and seated him at his right hand in the heavenly realms, far above all rule and authority, power and dominion, and every title that can be given, not only in the present age but also in the one to come. And God placed all things under his feet and appointed him to be head over everything for the church, which is his body, the fullness of him who fills everything in every way."

But this good news is not the end of the story. Paul continues. He proclaims that these words do not apply only to Jesus. Incredible as it may seem, they apply to *us*. Read the following words from Ephesians 2:4-10 very carefully. Paul goes on to add: "But because of his great love for us, God, who is rich in mercy, made us alive with Christ even when we were dead in transgressions—it is by grace you have been saved. And God raised us up with Christ and seated us with him in the heavenly realms in Christ Jesus, in order that in the coming ages he might show the incomparable riches of his grace, expressed in his kindness to us in Christ Jesus. For it is by grace you have been saved, through faith—and this not from yourselves, it is the gift of God—not by works, so that no one can boast. For we are God's workmanship, created in Christ Jesus to do good works, which God prepared in advance for us to do."

Here Paul announces that in Christ we, too, have been exalted to the right hand of the throne of God with Christ. He states emphatically that this has nothing to do with our own works or goodness. We are exalted not because we are so deserving, but because God is so gracious. If we are only willing to accept the gift, Christ's victory is also our victory.

But, you say, now we are right back to square one. We have come full circle and are back to a position that doesn't square with reality. If I can't believe that I have dominion over everything, then surely you don't expect me to believe that I have been exalted to the very throne of God.

I remember one early winter morning

Souls are not entities that live within humans. Rather, human beings are souls in their total person. The body is not just a shell for the soul, but a part of the unified, indivisible person.

when I was teaching a college class in Paul's letters. It was that part of the winter when classes began before the sun came up. The students at that hour were a tired lot. I'm sure that some of them had dragged themselves out of bed in their dorm a few hundred feet away only five or 10 minutes before entering class. That morning the passage for study was Ephesians 2. I began by asking the class, "How many of you feel as if right now you have already been exalted to heaven and are at the right hand of the throne of God?" I've never had people look at me like I was so crazy.

But strange as it may seem, Paul's message is true. If we will only accept Him, Jesus Christ is our representative. We have to look at Him in all the glory of His victory over sin and death to see what human beings really are—to see what *we* really are. We are the children of God, those whom God wishes to have with Him at the throne of the universe.

Now it is true, of course, that this victory has not yet been fully realized, or put into effect. Paul shows that when he says that in the "coming ages" the full measure of God's grace will be shown. Paul teaches that this will come in the future when Jesus returns to this world to bring eternal salvation to all who have accepted Him as their Saviour (see 1 Thessalonians 4:13-18). But Christ's victory is so certain, and salvation is so sure, that Paul can speak of our exaltation as an already accomplished fact. He could never do this if salvation were based on our

For God so loved the world that he gave his one and only Son, that whoever believes in him shall not perish but have eternal life (John 3:16, NIV).

works or our worthiness. It is only possible because salvation is based on the completed victory of Jesus.

In other words, to answer the question Who are we? we have to look beyond our present line of sight. We have to look *up* to Jesus and *forward* to the future that He has promised us.

And that promise makes a difference *now*. It gives our lives new meaning and a new goal. We no longer need to feel dominated and defeated, for we know that we are God's children and that Christ has already secured our victory. We live with a new confidence and courage, undaunted by the little problems now that cannot be compared with the future that is ours.

Let's summarize then. The biblical picture of humans is an exalted one. Humans are creatures of God, made as His children and in His image to have dominion over the world. And even though humans have fallen through sin and have lost this dominion, Jesus Christ, the true human being, has gained the victory for them. His victory is so certain that Paul can already picture humans—us—as exalted to the throne of God in heavenly places. And that knowledge of our destiny, along with our present fellowship with God through Jesus, gives our life new meaning, so the words of Psalm 8 really are about us.

This means that any philosophy, either secular or religious, that depreciates the value of human life, or any aspect of it, must be rejected. Human life is good and valuable. It also means that any views or practices that damage human life in this world must be rejected.

> *To answer the question Who are we? we have to look beyond our present line of sight. We have to look **up** to Jesus and **forward** to the future that He has promised us.*

Bodily existence in this world is God's gift. It should be preserved and cared for. God has shown the value of human life by raising Jesus and exalting Him. Now that we know the value God places on our lives and the meaning that they have, all that we do should be consistent with that value.

One day while I was walking on a college campus, a bulletin board caught my attention. In big letters it asked the questions "Who are you? What are you all about? Read this sign and find out." Well, I read the sign, but I didn't find out. What I did find was a glowing promise about what I *would* discover if I would only fill out the card attached to the bottom of the poster and send it in along with $7. Then I would receive a personalized, computerized horoscope service that would analyze my character and tell me who I was and what I was all about.

Needless to say, I didn't send in the $7. How grateful I am that I don't need to rely on computerized horoscopes to tell me who I am! God's Word has already given me that good news. I am God's child. The glowing words of Psalm 8 are about me, because Jesus is my representative at the throne of God. Jesus is my Saviour, and in Him I find out who I am.

And however you may feel, these words in the psalm are about you, too, if you will only accept Jesus' free gift and let Him be your Saviour.

Of course, all this is based on an understanding of God as our Creator. We know who we are because we know we are His creatures. Yet in a modern scientific age, can we still trust the biblical notion that God is Creator? Let's look at that subject in more detail in our next chapter.

CHAPTER 11

More Than a Naked Ape

Years ago I used to pastor a church in San Diego, California. A large, beautifully colored stained-glass window stood at the front of the church above the pulpit. The eyes of anyone who sat in the congregation were immediately drawn to it.

I had seen it for the first time several years before I pastored there, when a college friend of mine was married in the church. My wife and I entered and sat down in one of the pews. It was evening, and the sun was just going down and shining through the window. Our eyes were immediately drawn to the magnificent beauty of the window. It looked like an abstract design of shapes and colors in a modern arrangement.

But as I continued looking, I noticed objects in the design. There was a flamingo near the bottom right-hand corner. That aroused my curiosity, and I began wondering if there were other objects there as well.

> *Any philosophy, either secular or religious, that depreciates the value of human life, or any aspect of it, must be rejected.*

94

Soon I saw some stars and a moon. There were things that looked like fish and animals, and finally toward the bottom of the picture I noticed two images that looked like human beings, a man and a woman. I turned and found out that my wife was doing the very same thing. Finally it dawned on both of us at the same time. We realized that this was not just a series of designs. It was a picture of the Creation story from the first part of the Bible, Genesis, chapter 1. It wasn't apparent at first glance, but eventually it became clear.

When I pastored that church, I saw the same scenario repeated over and over. It was fun to sit in front and watch the faces of those who were there for the first time. They would sit down, and their eyes would immediately be drawn to that stained glass window. I could see this serious expression on their faces as they tried to make out what it was in that picture. Finally the light would dawn, and I would enjoy seeing their smiles as they realized what this window was all about.

The Creation story itself is like a window—a window on ourselves and a window on God's plan for us. Once the light dawns, and we grasp its message, we learn even more about who we are and about God's plan for us. Let's take another look at this story.

The Bible begins with the following words: "In the beginning God created the heavens and the earth. Now the earth was formless and empty, darkness was over the surface of the deep, and the Spirit of God was hovering over the waters. And God said, 'Let there be light,' and there was light. God saw that the light was good, and he separated the light from the darkness.

After God's work on each day, Genesis tells us that God looked and saw that it was good.

God called the light 'day,' and the darkness he called 'night.' And there was evening, and there was morning—the first day" (Genesis 1:1-5).

It is important to notice several things right here in the beginning of the Creation story. First of all, the story certainly does not answer all the scientific questions that we in the twentieth century might wish that it did. I, for instance, don't know what it means when it says that the earth was "formless and empty." I can't give you a precise description of what the world was like in that state. What is clear is that Creation took place by God's action through His own word. God spoke, and what He called into existence came to be. That first day He called light into existence.

Open your own Bible to the first chapter of Genesis and read it through. Notice what God called into existence on each of the remaining days of Creation week. Let's look most carefully at the sixth day, the day God created human beings in His own image. "Then God said, 'Let us make man in our image, in our likeness, and let them rule over the fish of the sea and the birds of the air, over the livestock, over all the earth, and over all the creatures that move along the ground.' So God created man in his own image, in the image of God he created him; male and female he created them" (verses 26, 27).

After God's work on each day, Genesis tells us that God looked and saw that it was good. At the end of the sixth day, when God created human beings, verse 31 tells us that God looked and saw that it was *very* good. In other words, the Bible pictures the creation of human beings as something special.

But, of course, today many question whether human beings can really claim such a noble heritage. They say that human beings are simply the result of a long process of evolution and nothing more. I think of a book by Desmond Morris called *The Naked Ape*. Although his real agenda is to argue for ecological responsibility—certainly a good and much-needed agenda—he argues that human beings are nothing more than naked apes.

He says: "Despite our grandiose ideas and lofty self-conceits, we are still humble animals, subject to all the basic laws of animal behavior. . . . We tend to suffer from a strange complacency that this [the extinction of our species] can never happen, that there is something special about us, that we are somehow above biological control. But we are not. Many exciting species have become extinct in the past, and we are no exception. Sooner or later we shall go, and make way for something else" (p. 240).

Which is true? Who are we? Creatures of God made in His image, or mere naked apes, products of a chance process of evolution? And what is our destiny? To live with our Creator forever, or merely to make way for whatever species is next on the scene in our world?

First, let's notice the significance of the biblical picture. What difference does it make? Then we will turn to the question of whether this biblical picture is believable in a modern, scientific age. We must first realize that the purpose of the Creation story in the Bible isn't to satisfy all our historical and scientific curiosity about the origin of the world. If this were a scientific account, written in modern times, it would be very different. But as we've noticed in the previous chapter when we surveyed Psalm 8, the Bible's purpose is to tell us who we are and point us to God's plan for our salvation, both now and in the future.

God wants us to know through the Bible that we are

His creatures and that He has been acting for our salvation right from the beginning. In fact, Christ, who is His very Word, was the active agent in our creation. Jesus isn't just a newcomer on the scene brought in to rescue us when something went wrong. Christ was the active agent in our creation from the beginning.

Notice John 1:1-3: "In the beginning was the Word, and the Word was with God, and the Word was God. He was with God in the beginning. Through him all things were made; without him nothing was made that has been made."

It was God's Word who created us and our world in the very beginning. If you have any doubt about who this Word is, look in verse 14 of John 1, and see that the Word became flesh and lived for a while among us. This, of course, is a reference to Jesus Christ.

We see the same picture when we turn to Colossians 1. Referring to Jesus, Paul tells us: "He is the image of the invisible God, the firstborn over all creation. For by him all things were created: things in heaven and on earth, visible and invisible, whether thrones or powers or rulers or authorities; all things were created by him and for him. He is before all things, and in him all things hold together. And he is the head of the body, the church; he is the beginning and the firstborn from among the dead, so that in everything he might have the supremacy" (verses 15-18).

Let's add to this one more verse, Hebrews 1:1: "In the past God spoke to our forefathers through the prophets at many times and in

> *God wants us to know through the Bible that we are His creatures and that He has been acting for our salvation right from the beginning.*

various ways, but in these last days he has spoken to us by his Son, whom he appointed heir of all things, and through whom he made the universe."

The New Testament is clear that Christ is not only our Redeemer, not only our Saviour, not only coming again, but also that He is our Creator as well. We are His from the beginning. God made all things through Him. Our life, our breath, our existence, is a gift from Him.

So what difference does all this make? First of all, knowing that we are God's children gives our lives dignity and meaning. It keeps us from depreciating ourselves. It also binds us to our Saviour. It leads us to appreciate Him and praise Him. It keeps us from the folly of worshiping false gods. Paul shows in Romans 1:21-25 the utter folly of worshiping other objects that God has created, instead of worshiping the Creator Himself. Finally, knowing that we are all God's children, created in His image, gives us a deep appreciation for every other human being. It binds us together as brothers and sisters.

Thus we see a theological purpose and a practical purpose in the biblical account of Creation. This window on us and our world lets us know who we are, how we are related to other people and to God, and how we should worship.

But can we believe all this in a modern, scientific age? Can such a story make sense? First, let me admit that I'm not a scientist and would be lost in the details of scientific arguments. But there are some important,

> *Knowing that we are God's children gives our lives dignity and meaning. It keeps us from depreciating ourselves. It also binds us to our Saviour.*

general considerations that all of us—scientists or not—can understand. At this point I wish to focus on just two considerations. First, the *nature* of the scientific method, and second, the *evidence* of creative design that we see in our world.

The scientific method works from cause to effect. Scientists want to know what causes brought forth a certain state of affairs. To make valid deductions, scientists must assume a continuous, orderly system.

We all know that this method has served us well. Scientific knowledge is a wonderful blessing to all of us. It has enabled us to lengthen our life spans, to enter space, and to do all the helpful things that we do with our personal computers (including writing books like this). But there are limits to what the scientific method can be expected to do. To recognize that is not to depreciate science in any way. Recognizing limits is a part of good science.

If the scientific work we do in this world must assume a continuous orderly system of some sort (although even within that system scientists also recognize and account for certain kinds of chaos), science has no way of getting out of the system to talk about the beginning of the system. It must assume a continuous chain of cause and effect.

But how would you get outside that chain and ask how the whole system began? The answer is, simply, You can't. The

> *For by [Jesus Christ] all things were created: things in heaven and on earth, visible and invisible, whether thrones or powers or rulers or authorities; all things were created by him and for him (Colossians 1:16, NIV).*

scientific method cannot really answer the ultimate question of origin one way or the other. Scientists can offer theories, but these must be recognized as theories that can neither be proved nor disproved. Science can tell us a lot about the history of our world, but it can never find a place outside of that history where it can rule on the question of whether what is here is the result of chance or of God's plan. We will have to decide that question on the weight of evidence. Which makes the most sense? That brings me to the second consideration.

My wife is a nurse-midwife and has studied fetal development. When I look at the pictures in her books—actual photographs of the developing fetus—it is truly amazing how that tiny cell develops into a person. It is equally amazing that that person is born into an environment that will sustain life. The sun and moon are just the right distance from the earth. If the sun were a bit closer, we would burn; if it were farther away, we would freeze. If the moon were 50,000 miles away instead of 240,000, tides would inundate the whole world twice a day.

Which is easier to believe? That through an unbelievable, incredible series of happy coincidences all this just happened, or that an intelligent mind stands behind it? Creation cannot be proven scientifically, but neither can any other theory. I believe that this biblical window makes the most sense. It explains in the best way the facts as we actually see them, and it gives me the best understanding of who I really am.

I once spent a weekend on a retreat

God is our Creator and He loves us. He has a plan for our lives, and all the people of the world are His children, our brothers and sisters.

with a group of church members. Every service began with a time of singing, and the leader always began by asking if anyone in the group had a favorite song he or she wanted to start off with. At every meeting, the same thing happened. One cute little boy, hardly old enough to talk, would raise his hand first and say, "I want two songs, 'Jesus Loves Me,' and 'Jesus Loves the Little Children.' " And so we would sing his two favorites.

Not a bad combination. That is precisely what this window of the Creation story reveals. God is our Creator and He loves us. He has a plan for our lives, and all the people of the world are His children, our brothers and sisters.

We now turn to two special gifts that God has given to human beings—gifts that are introduced in this Creation story as part of the very first book of the Bible. The next chapter focuses on the gift of marriage and family, and the following two chapters look at the gift of Sabbath.

> *By the word of the Lord were the heavens made, their starry host by the breath of his mouth. . . . For he spoke, and it came to be; he commanded, and it stood firm (Psalm 33:6-9, NIV).*

CHAPTER 12

Is the Family Obsolete?

As I write, the Christmas season has just ended. One of the great joys of life is giving gifts to those whom you love. I remember the very first Christmas after our daughter, Laura, was born. She was just a few months old. We had gotten some simple things that we thought she would enjoy, and it was so much fun on Christmas morning to have her tear into the ribbon and paper. Of course we had to help her open the toys, but we found that when she got them open, she didn't really care about them. She was much more interested in the ribbon and the papers. We could have forgotten about the toys and just given her the wrappings! Laura is now 25 and in graduate school, but she still enjoys coming home for Christmas. Now, of course, she is interested in what is inside the packages, and not only does she enjoy the gifts we give her, but she always comes home with delightful and thoughtful gifts for us.

In the previous chapter we saw that God is our loving Creator and Parent. As such He, too, enjoys giving gifts. In fact, when we look more carefully at the Creation story that served as a basis for the previous chapter, we find two extremely important gifts that God gave to human beings right at the beginning to express His love.

God knew what human beings needed. After all, He made us. And because He loved us, He gave these important gifts to enrich our lives. These gifts are for our good. In this chapter we look at the first, and in the following two chapters we will turn to the second of these gifts that came from our loving Creator.

The first gift is one that affects every single one of us in one way or another. It is the gift of marriage and family. In Genesis 2:7 the Creation story tells us: "The Lord God formed the man from the dust of the ground and breathed into his nostrils the breath of life, and the man became a living being." Here we see the creation of Adam. But as we read on, we find that God did not consider His work complete when Adam was alone. In fact, He said it wasn't good for Adam to be alone.

Let's read the whole story in verses 15-24: "The Lord God took the man and put him in the Garden of Eden to work it and take care of it. And the Lord God commanded the man, 'You are free to eat from any tree in the garden; but you must not eat from the tree of the knowledge of good and evil, for when you eat of it you will surely die.' The Lord God said, 'It is not good for the man to be alone. I will make a helper suitable for him.' Now the Lord God had formed out of the ground all the beasts of the field and all the birds of the air. He brought them to the man to see what he would name them; and whatever the man called each living creature, that was its name. So the man gave names to

> *God did not want humans to be alone, and so He gave the gift of marriage and family.*

104

all the livestock, the birds of the air and all the beasts of the field. But for Adam no suitable helper was found. So the Lord God caused the man to fall into a deep sleep; and while he was sleeping, he took one of the man's ribs and closed up the place with flesh. Then the Lord God made a woman from the rib he had taken out of the man, and he brought her to the man. The man said, 'This is now bone of my bones and flesh of my flesh; she shall be called "woman," for she was taken out of man.' For this reason a man will leave his father and mother and be united to his wife, and they will become one flesh."

Here we find that God did not want humans to be alone, and so He gave the gift of marriage and family. Now, both Jesus (Matthew 9) and Paul (1 Corinthians 7) make it clear that not all will choose the gift of marriage. Some will find the single life better for them, and that is a legitimate Christian choice. In fact, it is a gift that God gives to some, and it is what is best for some. But most find this gift of marriage the state to which God calls them.

Notice several things about this gift from the passage we have just read. First, it meets the human need for companionship. Second, it involves leaving father and mother and forming a new home. Third, it involves a total oneness and commitment to each other that includes the sexual relationship as a symbol of that oneness. Fourth, Genesis 1:31 tells us that the creation of male and female was not only good, as was each day's creation, but it was *very* good. Finally, notice that it is God Himself who establishes this first marriage.

This gift of

> *This gift of marriage becomes one of the most important analogies for our understanding of God.*

marriage becomes one of the most important analogies for our understanding of God. As *children*, we learn of God through our parents' love and care. As *husband and wife*, we learn the meaning of faithfulness and commitment as we grow in a lifelong relationship together. As *parents*, we begin to sense how God must feel toward us as we realize that unique bond we have with our children. It's no accident that the Bible consistently uses analogies drawn from marriage and family to express our relationship with God. Home even becomes a foretaste of God's ultimate destiny for us.

But what we've just said is an ideal. We have only to look around in our world to know that in many cases, this ideal is far from reality. Instead of learning of God's love through their parents' love and care, many children suffer abuse. Instead of learning the meaning of faithfulness and commitment, many spouses find their marriages fractured by divorce.

This was never God's intention. In fact, because this gift was so valuable and because God had such high expectations for us, He protected this gift. He protected it through law. Now, you remember that in a previous chapter we talked about the law and saw that we can never earn our salvation by keeping the law. Rather, the law is God's gracious instruction that shows us how to live once we have accepted His free gift of salvation.

God knew that if we were going to enjoy the gift of marriage and family as He intended it, we would need to protect it and care for it. And so when we look at Exodus, chapter 20, and see the list of commandments that God gave His people to show them how to live, He included instruction about marriage. He said, "Thou shalt not commit adultery."

You see, God knew that if we were to enjoy this gift, we would have to appreciate it and commit ourselves to it, or it just wouldn't work. God knew that if the sexual relationship was going to be a symbol of oneness in a lifelong commitment of a man and a woman to each other, certain laws would be needed to preserve and protect that relationship. And so God not only forbids adultery in the Ten Commandments, but elsewhere He also calls on His followers to consider their marriage vows so sacred that they refrain from divorce. In fact, Jesus equates divorce and remarriage to another with adultery (Mark 10:11, 12).

This should make it clear that those who see law as a restriction of freedom simply misunderstand the point. God wants people to be free to enjoy the gift that He has given. He wants them to be free from problems that would detract from the gift. He knows that He created people to live the fullest and most enjoyable lives, and the gift of marriage can only reach its full capacity to bring human happiness when it is characterized by faithfulness, commitment, and permanence. So the law is given to protect and preserve.

That means when two people choose to marry, they enter into the joy and security that only a faithful commitment can ensure. They are no longer on trial. (In fact, the whole idea of trial marriage is an absurdity. The essential ingredient in marriage is commitment, and you can't have a trial commitment.)

It certainly doesn't take a genius to figure out that God's gift of marriage has been threatened today and that much of that threat comes because God's gracious instruction has been ignored. Today we are bombarded with a very different kind of message. The message says that sexuality is not limited to a committed marriage, but is, rather, acceptable as long as it is "safe." In other words, hygienically safe. But there is little emphasis on

107

what is morally safe according to God's plan.

Not long ago I was on a transcontinental movie flight. As the flight attendant came offering the headsets for the movie, hardly any of the people around me paid the money to rent them. It was night, and most passengers were either reading or sleeping. But it was interesting to see how powerful the visual images of the movie were. As I looked around, it was amazing that people who didn't have headsets and couldn't hear the words nevertheless tended to keep their eyes riveted on the screen. It is impossible to escape the constant bombardment of the media.

And the morality of the media couldn't be further from God's gracious instruction. But think about it. Which way do you think really leads to human happiness? Who really knows best? The God who created us and gave us the gift of family in the first place, or the wealthy exploiters of God's gift who use sex to sell everything from toothpaste to trucks?

Let's summarize what we have seen. At the very beginning when God created the world, He recognized that it wasn't good for human beings to be alone. He gave us the gift of family. At the core of family is a committed relationship between a man and a woman, a lifelong commitment that provides security for them and the right kind of nurturing for their children. It is God's will that faithfulness and permanence characterize marriage. This is so important that God protected the gift of marriage with gracious instruction. That's why the law contains the command "Thou shalt not commit adultery." It is also why we have the greatest potential for happiness when we take God's instruction seriously.

Before I close

> **When two people choose to marry, they enter into the joy and security that only a faithful commitment can ensure.**

this chapter, let me add a word to those who have found reading about God's ideal painful. Perhaps it is too late for you to experience this ideal. You have already suffered the trauma of divorce or have painful scars from experiences of abuse. Fortunately, the whole concept of a God of grace shows us that God never leaves us because of the experiences of the past. He continues to work to bring forgiveness for our past mistakes and healing for our wounds.

Think of the biblical example of David, who once killed a man to cover up an adulterous affair with the man's wife, and yet David was called a man after God's own heart. In this chapter we have focused on God's instruction, but we must remember that He is a God of forgiveness and healing as well.

We've now talked about the first of the two gifts that God gave at Creation. In the next two chapters we turn to the second gift.

It is God's will that faithfulness and permanency characterize marriage.

CHAPTER 13

God's Answer to the Problem of Stress

A number of years ago when my son was 13, I spent a summer teaching a group of ministers in Mexico. Both children went with me. It's a long drive from the Pacific Northwest to the university where we were headed, 200 miles south of the tip of Texas. In other words, it's a long time for an active 13-year-old to sit. But Larry had a lot of things to help him pass the time away. Sports games and baseball cards and the old standby, looking for license plates. Just a few miles away from our home in Walla Walla, we spotted a Rhode Island plate. That got him started. He began his list, and within a few minutes he also had Oregon, Washington, Idaho, Nevada, California, and most of the other states in the West. By the time we got to Mexico, he had seen 24 different license plates from the United States, plus some from Canada and Mexico. While we were in Mexico, he saw four more states, so when we started back, he had seen plates from more than half the country.

Our return trip was during the peak vacation season, and the plates came even more quickly. To top it off, on the way home we went through Yellowstone, a license plate collector's paradise. By the end of the first day there, Larry's list was up to 48, with just two more states to go—Hawaii and Delaware.

Would you believe that the next morning we saw a car from Hawaii? Now there was only Delaware left, and finding a license plate from Delaware became an obsession. He knew that once we left Yellowstone he wasn't likely to find it, and it would be a tragedy to go back home having seen 49 plates and missing just one state.

As our few days at Yellowstone went by, we heard more and more about Delaware. One morning when we got up, my wife offered Larry $5 if she wouldn't have to hear about Delaware until lunchtime. Within 10 minutes he had blown his $5! All we heard about was Delaware. When we went to see those magnificent sights like Old Faithful, Larry didn't bother to take a glance. He preferred to run up and down the parking lot, looking for a Delaware license plate.

Finally, the night before our departure, we went to Yellowstone Falls. Larry didn't want to see the falls. He wanted to stay and look for Delaware license plates in the parking lot. Talk about stress! Talk about anxiety! You would have thought that his whole life depended on finding a Delaware license plate!

We went to eat in a cafeteria near Yellowstone Falls. As we got out of the car to go in and get something to eat he begged, "Please, I

He gave us a weekly present that would give a rhythm to our lives and remind us of what is important and allow us freedom to find the rest and refreshment that we need.

don't want to eat. Can't I just stay out here and look for Delaware license plates?"

"No," we told him, "you have to eat."

So Larry went inside and ate as quickly as he could get the food down and then headed out to the parking lot. We went on in a leisurely way and finished our meal. When I had paid the cashier and was heading toward the door, here came Larry bounding across the parking lot. "Come here! You've got to see it! You won't believe it if you don't see it!"

All of us went running out, and there, just pulling out of a parking space, was a blue Volkswagen bus with a Delaware license plate. In fact, we got a picture, and even today, a decade later, when we look at our Yellowstone pictures, that picture tells more about what we did in Yellowstone than anything else.

It was amazing to me that such a simple little game, such an innocent endeavor, could become such an obsession, all-encompassing, all-consuming.

Unfortunately, many of us live our lives a lot like that. We are obsessed with some work or task or endeavor that keeps us in a continual state of stress, with little time for relaxation, recreation, or serious reflection.

God never wanted our lives to be like that, and way back at the creation of the world, because He knew us, because He loved us, and because He knew what was best for us, He gave us another gift. In addition to the gift of marriage and family that we talked about in the previous chapter, He gave us a weekly present that would give a rhythm to our lives and

> *Observe the Sabbath day by keeping it holy, as the Lord your God has commanded you (Deuteronomy 5:12, NIV).*

remind us of what is important and allow us freedom to find the rest and refreshment that we need.

This gift is also found in Genesis, chapter 2. Notice the first three verses: "Thus the heavens and the earth were completed in all their vast array. By the seventh day God had finished the work he had been doing; so on the seventh day he rested from all his work. And God blessed the seventh day and made it holy, because on it he rested from all the work of creating that he had done."

When God came to the end of His work, He rested. Now, obviously God doesn't get tired and need to rest. He did it for a purpose. He did it to set aside each seventh day of the week, each Sabbath, as a special gift just for us.

There are several reasons for this gift. First, God wanted us to remember who we are, that we are His creation. It's easy to get wrapped up in the hustle and bustle of a busy world and forget that we are God's children.

Second, God wanted people to spend time with Him. He knew that humans would find their greatest joy in continuous fellowship with Him. But that fellowship takes time, and so He said, "Let Me give you a day free from work during which we can spend time together." In other words, this gift is really an invitation.

Third, God knew that we would need time for rest and refreshment. We live best when we recognize that life is more than working, striving, achieving, and the usual stress and strain of life.

And so, for all these reasons, God gave us the gift of the Sabbath. But just as He needed to protect and preserve the gift of marriage with gracious instruction or law, He did the same for the Sabbath. Now, remember we've already seen that the purpose of law is not to earn God's favor but to enhance our lives when we have recognized God's grace and responded in love to Him. The law shows us the best way to live. And so God protected His gift of marriage with law, and He protected the gift of the Sabbath with law.

Here is what God says about the Sabbath in the Ten Commandments, found in Exodus 20:8-11: "Remember the Sabbath day by keeping it holy. Six days you shall labor and do all your work, but the seventh day is a Sabbath to the Lord your God. On it you shall not do any work, neither you, nor your son or daughter, nor your manservant or maidservant, nor your animals, nor the alien within your gates. For in six days the Lord made the heavens and the earth, the sea, and all that is in them, but he rested on the seventh day. Therefore the Lord blessed the Sabbath day and made it holy."

In order to preserve this gift so that it can accomplish its purpose, God knew that we would need to be free of work on this special day. Instead, we would devote the day to worship and rest and fellowship. God says this is to apply to the whole household. On Sabbath all are equal—servant and master, employee and employer, children and parents—all take time away from their normal work to remember their Creator, to rest and to recognize what is really important in life.

In Deuteronomy 5 we find a second giving of the Ten Commandments. Here the command is similar but with a little bit of difference that is worth noticing.

"Observe the Sabbath day by

> *God wanted people to spend time with Him. He knew that humans would find their greatest joy in continuous fellowship with Him.*

keeping it holy, as the Lord your God has commanded you. Six days you shall labor and do all your work, but the seventh day is a Sabbath to the Lord your God. On it you shall not do any work, neither you, nor your son or daughter, nor your manservant or maidservant, nor your ox, your donkey or any of your animals, nor the alien within your gates, so that your manservant and maidservant may rest, as you do. *Remember that you were slaves in Egypt* and that the Lord your God brought you out of there with a mighty hand and an outstretched arm. Therefore the Lord your God has commanded you to observe the Sabbath day" (verses 12-15).

God asks His people in the Old Testament to keep the Sabbath not only because of Creation, but also because He is the one who rescued them from slavery. The Exodus from Egypt, when God took His people who had become slaves and miraculously led them out to the Promised Land, is the great symbol of God's saving power in the Old Testament. And so here we see that the Sabbath helps people remember their Saviour as well as their Creator. The Sabbath reminds us that God is both Creator and Saviour.

God wants us to accept this gift and treat the Sabbath as a holy day, refraining from work and enjoying the benefits that come from this special gift. Unfortunately, just as the family has been threatened, this gift, too, has been undermined. Most of the Christian world today has turned away from the observance of the seventh-day Sabbath and is missing out on the blessing that God wants to give. This change has been

> *Jesus Christ is the one who gave us the Sabbath. In addition, when He was here on this earth, He worshiped on Sabbath.*

defended on many grounds, none of which stands up under close scrutiny.

Some have said that Sabbath is merely a Jewish ceremony. And yet notice that God gave this gift right at the Creation, long before the Jews as a people came on the scene.

Others have said that the Sabbath was superseded by Jesus, but remember that when we studied the Creation story two chapters back, we saw that it was actually the Word who became flesh and lived among us who was the Creator. In other words, Jesus Christ is the one who gave us the Sabbath. In addition, when He was here on this earth, He worshiped on Sabbath. Luke 4:16 tells us, "He went to Nazareth, where he had been brought up, and on the Sabbath day he went into the synagogue, as was his custom. And he stood up to read." Now, He didn't keep Sabbath in the same way as the Jewish leaders of His day. He objected to many of their legalistic rules about Sabbath and used it as a day to bring healing and salvation to people. But nevertheless, Jesus kept it.

Others object that it doesn't matter what day we keep as long as we keep one in seven. But there are several problems with this. First, God specifies one day. He says that the seventh day is the Sabbath. I think He did that for a reason. He knew that the day would stay more meaningful if we kept it as an anniversary of His Creation. Anniversaries just aren't the same when they're celebrated on different days. The fact is, it is the day that makes it special. It's been interesting to see in American tradition that when we lose the specificity of an anniversary, we also tend to lose its meaning.

Not long ago I went to the bank to get some money, only to be surprised that it was closed. It was a holiday, one of those holidays that we now celebrate on Monday, and except for banks and the post office no one even remembers what the day is for. God wants us to celebrate the Sabbath as a specific anniversary of His creating and saving.

As Christian worship has forgotten the seventh-day Sabbath, this inevitable shift has occurred. No longer is the day kept sacred. Sunday has become a day for Christians to go to church in the morning, but there is no sense of a full day of rest and worship in most of the Christian world. I think that's at least partially because we have gotten away from the specific celebration of Sabbath that the Bible teaches.

Finally, there are some who argue that the New Testament has changed the Christian day of worship from Sabbath to Sunday. Were this true, our commitment to the Bible would certainly necessitate such a change. But is it really true? This question is sufficiently important that we shall devote an entire chapter to it.

> *[Jesus] went to Nazareth, where he had been brought up, and on the Sabbath day he went into the synagogue, as was his custom (Luke 4:16, NIV).*

CHAPTER 14

The Difference a
Day Makes

When our kids were in college they had the best of both worlds. They lived in the college dormitory and had all the fun of dormitory life with their friends. But they attended the college where I teach—just two miles from home. When they got tired of cafeteria food, they could come home and have a meal whenever they wanted it. Sometimes they would even call home to find out what was on the menu for the night, and then decide whether the cafeteria would be better than that.

They also came home to do laundry. They were both very good about doing it themselves, however, and not just leaving it for Mom and Dad. But one night Laura didn't have time to finish. She left with the laundry in the dryer. My wife said that she would fold it and send it with me to school the next day. Laura could pick it up in my office.

My wife fulfilled her part of the bargain, but she had to leave very early for work the next morning. While I was still half asleep, she reminded me, "Be sure to take

Laura's laundry. She needs it, and she'll pick it up at the office today."

When I got up I actually remembered. But I was running a little late. It was time to leave the house, and so I went to get the laundry. Just one problem. I couldn't find it. I assumed it would be in the laundry room, but it wasn't there. I started searching the house for it.

Larry was still in high school at the time, and I was taking him to school on the way to the office. He stood by the door and was getting more and more impatient. "You've gotten me to school late so many times—one more time and I'm going to have to sit in detention for an hour. Now come on. Let's go!"

But I knew I had to find those clothes, and I kept on searching until finally he was adamant. I had to give up and leave without them. We left the house, but when we walked into the garage, there were the clothes sitting on the hood of the car. My wife wanted to make sure that I wouldn't forget.

I couldn't be too unhappy with her. The fact is that 99 percent of the time, I do forget. But it was very frustrating to spend all that time looking for something that wasn't there.

In this chapter we're going to spend time doing just that, looking for something that isn't there. You see, there are many people who believe that the New

> *Many people believe that the New Testament changed the day of worship from Sabbath, the seventh day of the week, to Sunday, the first day of the week. In this chapter we will look at every place in the New Testament that mentions the first day of the week to see if this is really true.*

Testament changed the day of worship from Sabbath, the seventh day of the week, to Sunday, the first day of the week. In this chapter we will look at every place in the New Testament that mentions the first day of the week to see if this is really true. When we're through, I think you'll see that we've been looking for something that simply isn't there. In each case we will begin by quoting the text, then discussing it.

The Resurrection Narrative

The first four passages that mention the first day of the week are parallel to each other. All four Gospels tell the story of Jesus' followers coming to the tomb on Sunday morning after Jesus' resurrection. They read as follows:

"After the Sabbath, at dawn on the first day of the week, Mary Magdalene and the other Mary went to look at the tomb" (Matthew 28:1).

"When the Sabbath was over, Mary Magdalene, Mary the mother of James, and Salome bought spices so that they might go to anoint Jesus' body. Very early on the first day of the week, just after sunrise, they were on their way to the tomb" (Mark 16:1, 2).

"On the first day of the week, very early in the morning, the women took the spices they had prepared and went to the tomb" (Luke 24:1).

"Early on the first day of the week, while it was still dark, Mary of Magdala came to the tomb. She saw that the stone had been moved away from the entrance" (John 20:1, REB).

Notice that we find nothing about a day of worship in any of these texts. In fact, it is significant that the women waited until the first day of the week to come to anoint Jesus' body. They, of course, were observing the seventh day of the week, the Sabbath, and so they waited until it was over to come to the tomb for Jesus' anointing. At least that's what they had in mind before they found out that He was risen.

In biblical times, the day began at sundown. The first part of the day was evening, and then the light part of the day was the last part of the day. (Remember the language of Genesis 1 that we saw a few chapters ago: it was evening and morning, the first day.) The women came early in the morning, perhaps when it was still dark, the early part of the first day of the week, on Sunday morning, to anoint Jesus' body. But these texts say nothing about a change in the day of worship.

John 20: Meetings With the Disciples

"On the evening of that first day of the week, when the disciples were together, with the doors locked for fear of the Jews, Jesus came and stood among them and said, 'Peace be with you!' After he said this, he showed them his hands and side. The disciples were overjoyed when they saw the Lord. Again Jesus said, 'Peace be with you! As the Father has sent me, I am sending you.' And with that he breathed on them and said, 'Receive the Holy Spirit' " (John 20:19-22).

In this passage we see the reason Jesus appeared to His disciples. But there is absolutely nothing here about a day of worship. In fact, the disciples were gathered, not for worship, but out of fear. They were hiding and didn't even know that Jesus was risen. Then Jesus appeared to let them know that He was alive.

In verse 26 we find that Jesus met with the disciples a week later. Thomas was not present in the first meeting and would not believe until he actually saw Jesus. Since this resurrection appearance was a week later, we can assume that it, too, was on Sunday, but the text doesn't say so specifically, nor does it make any point of the fact that this was the first day of the week. Nor again is there any suggestion that this was a day of worship. John 20 does nothing to call attention to Sunday as a new day of worship.

Acts 20: Paul's Preaching

"On the first day of the week we came together to break bread. Paul spoke to the people and, because he intended to leave the next day, kept on talking until midnight. There were many lamps in the upstairs room where we were meeting. Seated in a window was a young man named Eutychus, who was sinking into a deep sleep as Paul talked on and on. When he was sound asleep, he fell to the ground from the third story and was picked up dead. Paul went down, threw himself on the young man and put his arms around him. 'Don't be alarmed,' he said. 'He's alive!' Then he went upstairs again and broke bread and ate. After talking until daylight, he left. The people took the young man home alive and were greatly comforted" (Acts 20:7-12).

Here we find a passage that is used very frequently by those who believe that the New Testament changes the day of worship. After all, we read here about people gathered to break bread on the first day of the week.

But there are several things we need to notice here. Remember that the Jewish people reckoned the beginning of each day at evening, and this meeting was at night. The first day of the week—at night—would, according to this way of keeping time, be Saturday night. In fact, the *New English Bible* translates the

> **In biblical times, the day began at sundown.**

passage this way. It reads, "On the Saturday night, in our assembly for the breaking of the bread." So this was not what we would think of as a Sunday worship service, but rather a Saturday night meeting.

A second thing to notice is that according to Luke's account in the book of Acts of the early history of the church, Christians at that time broke bread every day. "Every day they continued to meet together in the temple courts. They broke bread in their homes and ate together with glad and sincere hearts" (Acts 2:46). Thus the fact that Paul and Christians were breaking bread together does not indicate a worship day at all.

There is still another interesting point to notice in this story. Paul preached until daylight. When he was through preaching, he left on a journey. If this is Saturday night and Paul preached until daylight, it means he preached until Sunday morning, and then he took off on a journey. Thus he hardly appears to have been observing Sunday as his day of worship.

When we consider all these facts—that they broke bread every day, that this was a Saturday night meeting, and that Paul began traveling the next morning—we hardly get the idea that this text supports a change of the day of worship from Sabbath to Sunday.

1 Corinthians 16: The Collection

"Now about the collection for God's people: Do what I told the Galatian churches to do. On the first day of every week, each one of you should set aside a sum of money in keeping with his income, saving it up, so that when I come no collections will have to be made" (1 Corinthians 16:1, 2).

In this passage Paul is speaking to the church members at the city of Corinth. He is planning on visiting them soon, and he wants to give them some advice.

Some argue that Paul must be talking about worship on the first day of the week, since he is discussing an offering, which is usually part of Christian worship services. But when we look at the passage carefully, there is no worship service to be found. Paul is speaking to people individually. He is telling them to set aside money on the first day of the week so that when he comes, they won't have to collect offerings and hear fund-raising appeals. They will already have money to contribute when he arrives.

Why did he ask them to do it on the first day of the week? We don't know, but clearly he doesn't say anything about a worship service. The implication is that they will do this at home. Perhaps he mentions the first day of the week because he wants them to do it right at the beginning of the week before they spend money on anything else. But there is absolutely no reference here whatsoever to a change in the day of worship.

Revelation 1: The Lord's Day

"I, John, your brother and companion in the suffering and kingdom and patient endurance that are ours in Jesus, was on the island of Patmos because of the word of God and the testimony of Jesus. On the Lord's Day I was in the Spirit, and I heard behind me a loud voice like a trumpet" (Revelation 1:9, 10).

In this passage there is no reference to Sunday or the first day of the week. Some, however, have identified the expression "the Lord's day" with

When Jesus and the religious leaders of His day disputed over how the Sabbath should be kept, Jesus affirmed the value of the Sabbath for human beings. He refused to make Sabbath a day of legalistic rules.

Sunday and, therefore, point to this passage as evidence for a change in worship.

It is true that later Christianity used the term "Lord's day" with reference to Sunday, but there is no evidence of that in the New Testament or during the first century. In this passage, John may not be speaking about a specific day at all. Perhaps he is referring to the Lord's day as the day of final judgment when Jesus will return. From the evidence in the text itself, it cannot be proved or disproved. There is no evidence here, however, that John is referring to the first day of the week, or to any other weekday for that matter.

Summary

We have just looked at all the passages in the New Testament that give any hint of the first day of the week. Would you agree that we've been looking for something that isn't there?

The change from worship on Sabbath, the seventh day of the week, to worship on the first day of the week actually came much more slowly in the Christian church. There is no evidence for it in the New Testament. Rather, there was a gradual elevation of the first day of the week, particularly in the early Christian communities of Rome and Alexandria, and along with it a gradual turning away from Sabbath that occurred as many Christians of Gentile origin did not wish to be associated with Jews at a time when Jews were unpopular.

The process took a couple of centuries and was much quicker in some locations than others. But if the Bible is our guide, it is very clear that God's invitation to devote the seventh day as the Sabbath to worship was never changed.

Let's close by looking at one more passage. "Then he [Jesus] said to them, 'The Sabbath was made for man, not man for the Sabbath. So the Son of Man is Lord even of the Sabbath' " (Mark 2:27, 28).

When Jesus and the religious leaders of His day disputed over how the Sabbath should be kept, Jesus affirmed the value of the Sabbath for human beings. He refused to make Sabbath a day of legalistic rules. His many encounters with the religious leaders of His day in the Gospels make that clear. But His dispute with them was always over *how* to observe the Sabbath, never over *whether* the Sabbath was valid. Jesus said that Sabbath is good for human beings. It was made for human beings, and Jesus also affirmed that He Himself was Lord of the Sabbath.

If the Sabbath were unrelated to Jesus, it would be meaningless. But it is Jesus Himself who invites us to take advantage of this gift that solves the problem of human stress and restlessness by providing rest, refreshment, and the spiritual energy that can come only from fellowship with our Lord Jesus Christ.

We now turn our attention to one of God's gifts that is more recent. Unlike marriage and the Sabbath, which came from the very creation of the world, this gift has come with Jesus' advent, but it is no less important.

CHAPTER 15

Why Should I Join a Church?

Many years ago, when I was living in southern California, I frequently had occasion to drive from Los Angeles to Riverside (a trip of about 60 miles) in the early morning. Fortunately, I was going in the right direction. Most of the cars traveled toward Los Angeles at that time of the day. Thus while I had smooth sailing, I had only to look to my left across the center divider to see the world's longest parking lot—miles of cars, thousands of them, inching along the San Bernardino Freeway, at times five lanes wide, trying to get into the city.

In addition to being grateful about driving in the right direction, I found it amazing that virtually each of these thousands of cars bore only one occupant. Certainly many of those drivers had departure points and destinations near each other—yet they drove one to a car.

Since that time city authorities have renewed efforts to encourage carpooling. They have assigned special lanes for cars with multiple occupants. But still the majority of rush-hour vehicles carry only a driver, with no riders.

I suppose that all this illustrates one of America's most important values—individualism. Most of us want to be free to come and go as we please without worrying about whether someone else is ready on time. We are a nation of individualists.

This value of individualism has had its effect on our religious understanding as well. We place great emphasis on the individual and his or her relationship to God. In fact, this emphasis often comes at the expense of a clear understanding of the church. It is popular to cry out against the dangers of "churchianity" and stress that people are not saved by being members of a church, and of course this is true. We sing "Not my mother, not my father, but it's *me*, O Lord, standin' in the need of prayer." And it is certainly true that we can never ride on anyone else's coattails into God's kingdom.

But our individualistic outlook carries certain dangers, too, for the New Testament strongly underscores the importance of the community of believers. There we find that Christianity is not just a matter of the single individual and his or her relationship to God. To accept Christ is to enter into a new, personal relationship with Him, but it is even more than that. It also includes entering into a new relationship with others who have also accepted Him.

Nowhere is this seen more vividly than in Paul's analogy of the body in 1 Corinthians 12. (It would be helpful if you would read this chapter, especially verses 12-27, for what

> *To accept Christ is to enter into a new, personal relationship with Him, but it is even more than that. It also includes entering into a new relationship with others who have also accepted Him.*

we are about to say is based upon it.) Here Paul compares us, as individual Christians, with the members of a body.

We are not simply individuals who have accepted Christ as our Saviour. We are also related to one another. We are not all the same. We have different gifts or talents (see verse 12), but our common bond with Christ binds us together into what Paul calls a body. This analogy says much about the purpose and necessity of the church.

Several implications follow from Paul's argument:

1. We need the body. Whatever our gifts, talents, or background, we remain inadequate by ourselves. The call to follow Christ includes a call to service. Yet none of us has all the talents necessary to fulfill the task. Only by pooling our gifts and working together can we successfully carry out our task.

Elsewhere in his letter (see 1 Corinthians 3:5-9), Paul shows that this had even been true in his own ministry for the Corinthians. God had used both Paul and Apollos in reaching the Corinthian people with the gospel. Paul had planted, Apollos had watered, and God had used their efforts to produce growth.

God can use our combined efforts as well. Some of us are hands, some are feet, some are ears, and some are eyes. Our ability to function depends upon our relationship to the body as a whole.

All too often we ask what we get out of going to church. When that question becomes dominant in our lives, we conclude that the preaching or the choir is not really all that good, and we decide to stay home. But, according to Paul, we need the body in order to

Christ is the head of the church, his body, of which he is the Savior (Ephesians 5:23, NIV).

fulfill our service for Christ.

2. The body needs us. Whatever our gifts, talents, or background, we are essential to the body. Paul reminds us how silly it would be for the ear to feel useless to the body because it couldn't see, or for the eye to feel useless because it couldn't hear. The body needs all its parts, and the church needs the gifts of every follower of Christ.

When Paul, in Romans 12:4-8, gives another list of the various gifts that members bring to the church, he includes not only the obvious needs—such as preachers, teachers, and administrators—but even includes those who have the ability to help others by their cheerfulness. The body needs all kinds of members. It needs every believer.

When we go it alone and decide to follow Christ without becoming an integral part of His church, we deprive the body of one of its members. And we must remember that this body is Christ's own body. It is the instrument that He uses to carry out His work in the world, just as He used His own physical body when He was here in this world. To deprive the body of our gifts is to deprive Christ. Too easily we forget that fact in our individualistic culture.

3. Through our membership in the body, we grow in our relationship with Christ. We not only have opportunity to use our gifts for service in the body, but also we grow closer to Christ by

Let us not give up meeting together, as some are in the habit of doing, but let us encourage one another—and all the more as you see the Day approaching (Hebrews 10:25, NIV).

our mutual fellowship.

This fellowship helps us develop love, patience, and compassion. We join in such close communication with others that when one member suffers, the whole body suffers; and when one member rejoices, the whole body rejoices (see 1 Corinthians 12:26). Christ uses this close, caring fellowship to help us develop a character that is more like His.

He uses it also to help us enjoy and understand His love for us. The loving concern that we receive from fellow members of the body becomes a symbol of Christ's concern for us.

Thus we see that for Paul the church is part of our relationship with Christ. There can never be any dichotomy between an individual relationship with Christ on the one hand and being part of the church on the other. The two go inseparably together.

Probably the most frequent objection to this picture grows out of the church's failure to live up to this ideal. All too often we fail to see a perfect demonstration of mutual concern and service for Christ in the church. And so people excuse their lack of involvement with the church by pointing to the hypocrites in the church or to the mistakes of church leaders.

But we should realize that a body made up of human beings—even human beings who have accepted Christ and put their trust in Him—will be an imperfect body.

How could it be otherwise? I am certainly aware of my own imperfections. If I am imperfect, can I expect perfection from the other parts

> *A body made up of human beings—even human beings who have accepted Christ and put their trust in Him—will be an imperfect body.*

131

of the body? The fact that the treasure of the gospel is "in earthen vessels" (2 Corinthians 4:7, RSV) shouldn't make us forget what a valuable treasure it is. In my physical body I am grateful for my eyes, in spite of their myopia and astigmatism. I am grateful also for my fellow believers in Christ. Like me, they are imperfect, but together we learn and grow in Christ.

The body is only one of several analogies that Paul uses to show the privilege and necessity of the church. Another graphic one is the family. Paul says that we are members "of the household of God" (Ephesians 2:19, RSV). Certainly none of us lives in a perfect family, and yet what a blessing it is to live as part of a family.

One Labor Day morning our family took advantage of the holiday and slept in just a bit. We were also dog-sitting for friends who had left town for the weekend. The dog, which had been very quiet the whole weekend, stayed in the garage right underneath our bedroom. Suddenly we all awoke with a start as we heard first a soft growl, then a noisy bark.

We hopped out of bed and peered out the window just in time to see a very frightened little girl running away from the garage window. It didn't take very long to figure out what she was up to. She had a teddy bear under her arm and a backpack over her shoulder. A piggy bank protruded from the top of the backpack. Obviously she was running away from home. We watched her run out across a field toward the road and decided to see whether we could help.

By the time we

> *None of us ever outgrows the need for family. And the very same thing is true in our relationship with Christ. He doesn't want us to be alone.*

dressed and rushed outside, the little girl was walking along the side of the road. When we walked up to her we received a friendly greeting. She gladly talked with us, but all questions about who she was and where she lived fell on deaf ears. The little girl had no intention of telling us—because she was running away from home.

Finally my wife—who is quite good at things like this—asked her whether she was old enough to know her telephone number. She seemed rather proud of the fact that she was, and recited the numbers one by one. I put them into my memory, walked into the house, dialed the number, and as gently and reassuringly as possible tried to find out whether the people on the other end of the line were missing a little girl.

At first they thought I was some crank caller. They assured me that their daughter was in her bedroom asleep—as they had been before I awakened them.

Finally I convinced them to take a look just to be certain. Sure enough, they discovered their little girl was missing.

They said they would be right over (they lived about a mile and a half away). By the time they arrived, the girl had come into our house to look at some kittens. As soon as she saw her parents drive into the driveway she ran and hid—she didn't want to go home. She was running away from home!

Her parents, wisely, didn't try to force her. Instead, they sat down and talked about the pancakes they were going to have in a little while and the fun things they were going to do on this day off work. Soon the girl emerged, and it was *her* idea to return home and rejoin the family.

I don't know what prompted the little girl to run away in the first place, but it didn't take long for her to find out that it was better to be part of her family than to wander alone with her backpack.

None of us ever outgrows the need for family. And the very same thing is true in our relationship with Christ. He doesn't want us to be alone. He not only offers us the gift of fellowship with Him, but He also gives us the privilege of participation in His family, the church. Although not a perfect family, it is far better to be part of its fellowship than to be alone.

As Paul reminds us: "Now you are the body of Christ, and each one of you is a part of it" (1 Corinthians 12:27).

The next chapter focuses on the special service God has provided as a means of symbolizing our entrance into this body.

> *And God placed all things under [Jesus'] feet and appointed him to be head over everything for the church (Ephesians 1:22, NIV).*

CHAPTER 16

Baptism— A Symbol of Belonging

On Sunday afternoon, August 30, 1964, at 4:00 in the afternoon, two significant events occurred in southern California. First, Ione and I stood in a sanctuary before a minister, recited vows to each other, and heard the minister say the words "I now pronounce you husband and wife." Second, there was an earthquake. Not a severe, damaging one, but strong enough that one could really feel the jolt just about the time we were walking into the church. We've always wondered if there might have been a relationship between those two events. It's one of those things that you don't think about very much.

We could, of course, have gotten married without having a ceremony in a church. After all, Tijuana wasn't all that far to the south, and Las Vegas to the east. We could have gone to a justice of the peace. But we felt that a wedding ceremony was a significant part of our decision to get married and commit ourselves to each other.

That wedding ceremony did several things. First, it gave us the opportunity to make a public commitment of our love for each other and of our decision to be loyal to each other. We decided that our love was not just a private matter, but something that we wanted to let the world know about. We wanted to let our friends know that we were committing our lives to each other so that they could give us moral support. There were friends who stood there with us. It was a time of public acknowledgment of our commitment to each other.

Second, the ceremony itself helped us better understand the significance of the step that we were taking that day. We met with the minister beforehand and counseled with him. We planned the ceremony. We stood there together and listened to the words of the minister and listened to the music. All these activities spoke to us of the significance of the step we were taking that day.

Finally, there was a very practical effect of having that ceremony to begin our marriage relationship. We met in college. Ione's parents lived 2,000 miles away, so we had relatives scattered all over the country. The wedding ceremony gave an opportunity for families to come together and meet for the first time. We each became part of the other's extended family. I met new aunts and uncles that day whom I didn't even know existed when I asked Ione to marry me, but since that time they have become a significant part of my life. You see, a new network of relationships, a new extended family was formed. We became part of new families. I was part of her family, and she was part of mine. And, of course, a new immediate family was formed.

Throughout this book we have been talking about another union of lives, the union of our life with Jesus Christ. God knows a picture is worth a thousand words, and so He has given us a ceremony somewhat analogous to a wedding ceremony to initiate that new relationship with Him. That ceremony is baptism. In fact, as I look at Scripture and see the purpose of baptism, it seems to me the purpose is very much like that wedding ceremony that began our marriage.

First, the service of baptism is a public acknowledgment of our commitment to Jesus Christ, our loyalty to Him, our recognition that He is the Lord of our lives. In Acts 2:36 Peter has just been preaching a sermon to the Israelites. He has been telling the Jews that the very Jesus Christ who was crucified, resurrected, and ascended was Lord.

Peter says: " 'Therefore let all Israel be assured of this: God has made this Jesus, whom you crucified, both Lord and Christ.' When the people heard this, they were cut to the heart and said to Peter and the other apostles, 'Brothers, what shall we do?' Peter replied, 'Repent and be baptized, every one of you, in the name of Jesus Christ for the forgiveness of sins. And you will receive the gift of the Holy Spirit. The promise is for you and your children and for all who are far off—for all whom the Lord our God will call' " (Acts 2:36-39).

When they came to recognize that Jesus was Lord, they asked, "What shall we do?" and Peter said, "Repent and be baptized." That baptism was a public acknowledgment of their commitment to Jesus as Lord. Peter also showed them that along with that command came a promise, that as they committed their lives to Jesus Christ, their sins would be forgiven and the Holy

The service of baptism is a public acknowledgment of our commitment to Jesus Christ, our loyalty to Him, our recognition that He is the Lord of our lives.

Spirit would be with them.

That brings us to the second purpose of baptism. It helps us understand what happens in our life when we give ourselves to Jesus Christ.

One of the most instructive New Testament passages in this regard is Romans 6. Paul isn't primarily talking about baptism in this passage. He is actually addressing the matter of whether Christians should go on sinning after they have accepted Christ (his answer is, of course, no). But in speaking to that question, he uses baptism as an example. From his illustration, we learn a lot about the meaning and purpose of baptism.

"What shall we say, then? Shall we go on sinning so that grace may increase? By no means! We died to sin; how can we live in it any longer? Or don't you know that all of us who are baptized into Christ Jesus were baptized into his death? We were therefore buried with him through baptism into death in order that, just as Christ was raised from the dead through the glory of the Father, we too may live a new life. If we have been united with him like this in his death, we will certainly also be united with him in his resurrection. For we know that our old self was crucified with him so that the body of sin might be done away with, that we should no longer be slaves to sin—because anyone who has died has been freed from sin. Now if we died with Christ, we believe that we will also live with him. For we know that since Christ was raised from the dead, he

When we are baptized, we are in a sense buried with Jesus Christ in death and then resurrected with Jesus Christ to a new way of life. In this sense, baptism is a miniature Passion play.

cannot die again; death no longer has mastery over him. The death he died, he died to sin once for all; but the life he lives, he lives to God. In the same way, count yourselves dead to sin but alive to God in Christ Jesus" (Romans 6:1-11).

Paul says that when we are baptized, we are in a sense buried with Jesus Christ in death and then resurrected with Jesus Christ to a new way of life. In this sense, baptism is a miniature Passion play. It's a reenactment of the death of Jesus Christ and the resurrection of Jesus Christ. A reenactment in which we ourselves are the actors and actresses who experience death and resurrection. A part of us dies—that part of us which rebelled against God, that part of us which took part in sin—and we are resurrected to a new kind of life. Not a perfect life that is free from any mistakes, but a life that has a new direction and a new focus.

It's something like the experience that an actor has when he plays a historic personage. The actor comes to understand the person he plays in a new way from the very act of representing that person.

When he was in junior high school, my son did a paper on Groucho Marx and participated in a skit featuring some of his humor. Larry really got into it. He didn't just study about Groucho Marx—he ate, slept, and breathed Groucho Marx. Even now, many years later, he felt compelled to watch when they had a Marx brothers movie marathon on one of the cable TV stations recently. In that exercise, he identified with Groucho Marx and came to understand him much better than if he had simply read about him.

In baptism, we identify with Jesus Christ. We enter the water of baptism to participate with Him in His death. We experience the fact that His death cleanses us from our sin. We come up out of the water, symbolizing our resurrection with Him. By participating, we come to understand more fully what Jesus means to us.

Third, the baptismal ceremony also creates a new extended family as we become a part of the body of believers. Remember the following verse from the previous chapter. "The body is a unit, though it is made up of many parts; and though all its parts are many, they form one body. So it is with Christ" (1 Corinthians 12:12).

Baptism introduces us as a new member of the body, a new member of God's own family. Through it we become part of a new network of relationships.

Do you see what I mean when I say that the baptismal ceremony is much like the wedding ceremony? It's a public acknowledgment of our commitment and loyalty to Jesus as Lord. It's an opportunity for us to reenact the death and resurrection of Jesus in a way that helps us understand it at a level that goes beyond words. And it's our entrance into that new family, Christ's body, the church. To accomplish all that, and I'm sure much more, Jesus invites us, when we come to Him, to take that public commitment of baptism.

There is a lot of confusion about baptism today, however, because in different religious communities baptism is performed in different ways. In some communities, infants are baptized shortly after they are born. In others, baptism occurs only when a person is old enough to make a decision. And in some religious communities, baptism

> *If baptism is going to be a symbol of our commitment, then it should be done only when we are able to make a commitment.*

actually means being dipped under the water and coming back up, whereas in others it just means a little bit of water being placed on the head. Does it make any difference *how* baptism is carried out?

I believe Scripture teaches that it does. Symbol and meaning are closely associated together in baptism. If baptism is going to be a symbol of our commitment, then it should be done only when we are able to make a commitment. A newborn infant isn't making a commitment. Someone else may want to dedicate that infant to God, but the infant itself cannot make a commitment, and that's why in the early church, baptism was always a matter of *decision*. It was 200 years into the history of the early church before we find infant baptism, and 400 years before it became a widespread practice. The Bible pictures baptism as an acknowledgment of commitment.

The manner of baptism is also important. If the symbolism represents death and burial with Jesus, and then resurrection with Him, it is only baptism by immersion which properly symbolizes that death and resurrection. Even to say baptism by immersion is a redundancy, because the word *baptism* means immersion, or to be immersed or dipped under. And whenever we read about actual baptisms in the New Testament, we find that it is important that the participants go into the water.

Let's look at two passages. The first pictures the baptism of Jesus. Obviously Jesus didn't need to be baptized for the forgiveness of His sins, because Jesus was sinless. But Jesus wanted to give us an example, and Jesus wanted fully to identify Himself with human beings. And so He was baptized by John, as we read in Mark 1:9-11: "At that time Jesus came from Nazareth in Galilee and was baptized by John in the Jordan. As Jesus was

141

coming up out of the water, he saw heaven being torn open and the Spirit descending on him like a dove. And a voice came from heaven: 'You are my Son, whom I love; with you I am well pleased.' "

Notice that Jesus comes up out of the water. He was immersed.

In John 3:23 we read that John the Baptist was baptizing in the River Jordan. If you look at the Jordan River today, there isn't a lot of water there. But notice where John chose to baptize in the Jordan. "Now John also was baptizing at Aenon near Salim, because there was plenty of water, and people were constantly coming to be baptized." John picked a place to baptize where there was plenty of water. He was not just sprinkling but baptizing in a way that required "plenty" of water.

The manner of baptism is important because it symbolizes the meaning of baptism—the manner and the meaning are related. Perhaps this will make more sense if you think about the flag of your country. The flag points beyond itself. It would hardly be correct to say that a flag is nothing more than a piece of cloth. The symbolism of the flag carries a special meaning to those who are loyal to the country for which it stands.

But let's say that next Flag Day I decide that I will display a flag outside my house. I decide, however, that I really like green better than red, and I'd rather have my stripes green. In addition, I like stripes that go up and down better than stripes that go sideways, so I'm going to make my stripes go up and down. I also think flowers will look

> *Jesus answered, "I tell you the truth, no one can enter the kingdom of God unless he is born of water and the Spirit (John 3:5, NIV).*

better in the corner than stars. I don't know if the new flag I'll display will be pretty or not, but one thing I do know—it won't be the flag of the United States. It will lack the meaning that makes it a symbol of our country. And baptism that isn't in keeping with the New Testament manner of baptism loses its meaning too.

Let's take the analogy of the flag a bit further. A number of years ago the Los Angeles Dodgers and the Chicago Cubs were playing a game in Dodger Stadium in Los Angeles. The national anthem was ringing out just before the game. As a flag was displayed on the field, someone from the stands ran down on the field and grabbed the flag and started to burn it. Rick Monday, then outfielder for the Chicago Cubs, rescued the flag from being burned. He became something of a hero in Los Angeles, and later played for the Dodgers.

When he ran to rescue the flag so that someone couldn't desecrate it, it didn't necessarily mean that he was a patriotic American, did it? It could be that he was a spy who was trying to fool us. In the same way, a person could go through the symbol of baptism and not actually make a commitment to Jesus Christ.

But let's look at it the other way. We would hardly, under any kinds of ordinary circumstances, view the person who desecrated the flag as a loyal and patriotic individual, would we? And if we are truly committed to Jesus Christ, how can we reject that special symbol which He has given us?

When my wife and I stood before the minister and heard him say "I now pronounce you husband and wife," it could be said that those were just words. But in fact, they were more than that. They pointed beyond themselves and created a new reality. Similarly, in a sense, we could say that a flag is just a piece of cloth, but we all know that it is much more than that. It is a symbol that points beyond itself to our country. And in a sense, one could say that the water in the baptistry of a church is just water, but Jesus Christ has made it much more than that. It, too, points beyond itself and becomes a significant moment in the life of the Christian that creates a new reality and introduces the new Christian to the body of Jesus Christ.

If you have not yet experienced the blessing of belonging symbolized by baptism, I invite you to consider it.

The remaining chapters in this book focus on what it is like to belong to a specific church.

> *All of you who were baptized into Christ have clothed yourselves with Christ (Galatians 3:27, NIV).*

CHAPTER 17

What Does God Expect of Me?

My college students are never more frustrated than when they don't understand an assignment. My wife can tell when I haven't been clear in giving an assignment, especially the night before it is due. She will turn to me and say, "The phone sure is ringing a lot tonight. Your students must have a test or a paper due tomorrow." And of course, the more uncertainty about the assignment, the more the phone rings.

Sometimes I deliberately design assignments to make special demands on my students' creativity. Afterward they often admit that these assignments have been rewarding for them, but during the process they feel frustrated. Almost all my students would prefer a specific list of items to memorize rather than an assignment that makes them think.

What all this means is that human beings like clear expectations. We don't like uncertainty, whether it is in school or at work. We like to know clearly what is expected of us.

It's this same tendency that leads a lot of people I

145

meet to feel frustrated in their spiritual life. They find it hard to be clear about God's expectations. What does God expect of me, anyway?

We hear all kinds of slogans, phrases, and admonitions. "Just have faith." "Be perfect." "Surrender your will." "Trust in God." "Obey." "Let go and let God." "Keep the Ten Commandments." "Trust." "Be good." "Love your fellowman."

What do these admonitions mean? And how in the world would we put them all together and come up with a clear understanding of what God really wants?

When we look around the world, we find people doing all kinds of activities in an attempt to please God and meet His expectations. Some walk through fire. Others live solitary lives. Yet others give money to place their names under stained-glass windows. Others beat their backs with steel-barbed whips. Still others say "I believe," and go cheerily on their way. What *is* it that God really wants from us?

One of the classic and most beautiful answers to this question is a very old one—about 2,700 years old. We find it in the book of Micah, who prophesied to Israel and Judah around 700 years before Christ. Micah received the unenviable task of rebuking God's people who had gone astray.

His rebuke centered on two specific aspects of their behavior. First, they had forsaken their commitment to the one true God, who had led them out of Egypt and formed them as a nation. They had turned to idols, images of wood and stone. The second problem concerned their relationships with others. The land was full of injustice and oppression.

"They covet fields and seize them, and houses, and take them. They defraud a man of his home, a fellowman of his inheritance" (Micah 2:2). "The godly have been swept from the land; not one upright man remains. All men lie in wait to shed blood; each hunts his brother with a net. Both hands are skilled in doing evil; the ruler demands gifts, the judge accepts bribes, the powerful dictate what they desire—they all conspire together" (Micah 7:2, 3).

Micah's reactions to these evils sometimes appear bizarre and drastic. After referring to Israel's idolatry, he says, "Because of this I will weep and wail; I will go about barefoot and naked. I will howl like a jackal and moan like an owl" (Micah 1:8). Micah then puts the people on trial and reads the indictment against them.

But in the course of this indictment and appeal, Micah gives an answer to the question What is it that God really wants? "With what shall I come before the Lord and bow down before the exalted God? Shall I come before him with burnt offerings, with calves a year old? Will the Lord be pleased with thousands of rams, with ten thousand rivers of oil? Shall I offer my firstborn for my transgression, the fruit of my body for the sin of my soul? He has showed you, O man, what is good. And what does the Lord require of you? To act justly and to love mercy and to talk humbly with your God" (Micah 6:6-8).

How are God's people to respond to the indictment against them? Are they to respond by bringing great gifts, making sacrifices, and performing works that will somehow win God's favor? Would it impress God with their piety if they even gave up their own children in sacrifice to Him? What does God want them to do?

> *He wants them to do only three things: to act justly, to love mercy, and to walk humbly with God.*

God's answer through Micah is simple, elegant, and clear. He wants them to do only three things: to act justly, to love mercy, and to walk humbly with God.

To act justly. What God expects of us cannot be separated from our relationship with others. Every person on this earth is one of His children—whether president or prisoner, corporate executive in a suite overlooking Park Avenue or street person huddled over a vent. The wealthy, the widows, young or old, male or female, Black or White—all are His children.

God cares how His children are treated. If you are a parent, you know that if anyone mistreats one of your children, the reaction inside you is even more intense than if they mistreat you. God cares about His children, and He expects us to treat each one with justice and fairness and compassion.

To love mercy. The Hebrew word that is translated mercy is a very difficult word to put in English. It's one of those rich words that mean far more than any single expression in another language can communicate. It is related to the concept of covenant. In ancient times life was seen as governed by an array of covenants that bound individuals to other individuals. The covenant of marriage bound husband and wife together. Other covenants were of a much less significant and more temporary nature—covenants that governed business

> **Micah shows us that what God really expects is an appreciative response to His goodness in which we recognize that we are His children, walk humbly with Him, and treat His other children with respect, fairness, and compassion.**

relationships, for example.

The word here translated mercy involves not only kindness but loyalty and commitment to one's covenants. Since the most important covenants of life involve a keeping love, that concept also is included in this single word. Words like loyalty, commitment, love, mercy, kindness, and responsibility are all bound up in this word. To love mercy is to act in a loving and responsible way toward both God and other people.

To walk humbly with God. God's people had forgotten that they owed their life as a nation as well as their individual lives to Him. He was their Creator and the one who had rescued them from slavery and made them a nation. He didn't demand great impressive acts to prove their devotion. He just wanted them to appreciate His gracious generosity to them, recognize Him as God, and walk humbly with Him. These few words say so much. They imply a continuing relationship and a stance of humility that recognizes that God is God and we are the creatures who owe Him everything.

Thus, Micah shows us that what God really expects is an appreciative response to His goodness in which we recognize that we are His children, walk humbly with Him, and treat His other children with respect, fairness, and compassion.

This sounds simple, yet it sums up what God has tried to say to us throughout the ages. Wherever we look, we find these same two basic elements—appreciation for God and respect for His children—clearly stated as God's expectation for us. For example, the Ten Commandments in Exodus 20 begin with an expression of what God has done for us. God says, "I am the Lord your God, who brought you out of Egypt, out of the land of slavery." After this proclamation of His saving grace, He goes on to

149

summarize His expectations of us.

The first four commandments emphasize our appropriate response to God—to recognize Him as God and walk with Him in worship. The last six commandments detail how we will respect God's other children.

Of course, throughout history some have misunderstood the nature of these provisions and have seen the law as a way to earn God's favor rather than as a response to His goodness.

Both Jesus and Paul the apostle sought to set the record straight in this regard. Jesus summarized the law in the two great commandments: love God with all your heart and love your neighbor as yourself. Here again we see the two basic elements included in Micah's words 700 years earlier. And Paul, who so clearly points out the danger of reliance on law rather than on God's grace for salvation, continually includes these same two fundamental principles.

For example, the first part of the book of Romans sets forth the great doctrine of salvation by grace through faith. It shows the appropriate response of human beings to God's goodness—a response of faith, trusting God, and walking with Him. But the last part of the book of Romans (from chapter 12 onward) speaks of the Christian's responsibility to other people.

Even Paul's strong expression of the doctrine of salvation by grace apart from works of law in Galatians 3

> *But the fruit of the Spirit is love, joy, peace, patience, kindness, goodness, faithfulness, gentleness and self-control (Galatians 5:22, 23, NIV).*

ends with the affirmation that God does not show partiality and that all—whether Jew or Gentile, male or female, slave or free—are one in Christ.

The expectations so beautifully stated in Micah 6 ring forth throughout God's Word. What is it that God wants? He wants an appropriate response to His gracious goodness, a commitment to Him that recognizes Him as our God, and a continual walk with Him in a life of devotion and worship. But there is more. He also expects responsibility toward others—a respect for each person as His child, a respect that demands fair and loving treatment for all.

God's expectations are not confusing. They are clear. It is true, they are demanding expectations. It may be heartening to know that we don't have to bring rivers of oil and thousands of animals to please God, but who of us is able to act justly and love mercy as we should? Lest these expectations discourage us, the book of Micah ends on a positive note.

It reminds us that the God who has these expectations is still the God of grace and goodness. He is a God who pardons sin and forgives our mistakes. He is a God who delights to show mercy.

How should we respond to such a God? How can we do anything else but walk humbly with Him and treat His children with respect?

> *Love is patient, love is kind. It does not envy, it does not boast, it is not proud. It is not rude, it is not self-seeking, it is not easily angered, it keeps no record of wrongs (1 Corinthians 13:4, 5, NIV).*

CHAPTER 18

Why We Are Seventh-day Adventist Christians

Throughout this book we have tried to examine what the Bible has to say about God's plan for us and for our world. We have emphasized the importance of following Christ and being part of His body. But today there are many different Christian denominations. How can one make a decision about which church to join?

In this final chapter, I want to share why I have chosen the Seventh-day Adventist Church. And for this final chapter, I have invited my wife to write with me. Our backgrounds and biographies are quite different, and I hope that this will be helpful for diverse readers.

None of us can ever separate our religious faith from our biographies. But that does not mean that our religious faith is merely an accident of our personal histories and the people and events that have shaped our lives. As we explain why we are Seventh-day Adventist Christians, for example, part of the answer has to do with our own biographies, but that is not the whole story. Another part lies in values, beliefs, and commitments that must be renewed throughout life.

Perhaps we can illustrate this interplay as the two of us, with quite different stories, share something of the biographies and the beliefs that have led us to become and remain Seventh-day Adventists.

First, a word about both of us collectively before we tell our individual stories. We have been married to each other for nearly 30 years—slightly more than half of our lives. John is a college administrator and religion teacher, and Ione is a certified nurse-midwife who delivers babies at two hospitals in our town. We have two children whose ages are 25 and 23.

John

My Seventh-day Adventist roots go back a long way. I'm a fourth-generation Adventist. My great-grandfather on my mother's side immigrated to the United States from Alsace-Lorraine in the 1860s. When he landed in Michigan, he read a tract by an early Adventist minister, Uriah Smith, and became convinced that the seventh day of the week, Saturday, was the scriptural day for Christian worship—the Sabbath.

So I was born into an Adventist Christian home, attended Adventist schools from the first grade through college, and started going to church long before I can remember. Several times during this process, I experienced periods of intense questioning and reevaluation of Adventism, but family, friends, and social structure would have made it much harder for me to decide *not* to be an Adventist than to stay in the church. For me, the question Why am I an Adventist? is really a matter of why

For me, the question Why am I an Adventist? is really a matter of why I have decided to remain an Adventist.

153

I have decided to *remain* an Adventist.

Ione

My story is quite different from John's. I came from a broken home. My parents divorced when I was 3 years old, and I lived with an aunt and uncle after it became too difficult for my father and grandparents to care for me and my brother. During my teenage years my father remarried, and eventually I moved in with him and my stepmother. Going to church during these years was a peripheral activity for our family. My parents claimed to be Christians, but religion wasn't a major consideration in their day-to-day lives.

When I was 16 and a sophomore in high school, I became acquainted with Adventists. A physician at the hospital where I worked as a nurse's aide and for whom I sometimes did baby-sitting invited me to attend some evangelistic meetings with his family. George Vandeman, founder of and at the time speaker for the *It Is Written* TV broadcast, conducted the meetings. As he preached, I committed my life to Jesus and decided to be baptized.

Coming home after the meeting one night, I found my father and stepmother talking in the kitchen. They told me that I could not become a Seventh-day Adventist and that I must not work for the Adventist physician and his wife anymore. I replied that although they could decide where I could baby-sit, they didn't have the right to dictate my religious beliefs.

At that my father became angry. He marched me into the garage, removed his Western belt, and began to strap me. It made him furious that

> *My parents claimed to be Christians, but religion wasn't a major consideration in their day-to-day lives.*

I wouldn't cry, so he turned his belt around and whipped me with the buckle end. I've always felt that the angels were protecting me at that point, because soon the buckle hit the wall and broke.

Searching for some other means of inflicting punishment, he picked up a stick of wood and beat me until it also broke. With each stroke, he asked if I was going to obey him. I told him that I would, but that I must obey God first. Eventually he grew exhausted and stopped—but not before I was covered with welts and bruises. Within a few weeks I was secretly baptized, and during the next two years attended church whenever I could do so without my father knowing.

Right after I graduated from high school my father told me that I would have to stop all religious activities or leave home. Two days later I moved out and began attending an Adventist college. That was more than 30 years ago. Despite numerous attempts to contact my father and reconcile matters with him, I've had only two brief contacts with him during those years.

Spiritual Benefits

Even though these two biographies and ways of coming to an Adventist Christian faith are so different, the reasons that *keep* both of us in that experience and faith are quite similar.

Both of us find many spiritual fringe benefits in Adventism that affect our whole way of life (we will say more about these later). First and foremost, however, we are not Seventh-day Adventists because of these benefits. Our primary reason is our conviction that the basic, fundamental beliefs of Adventism are based on Scripture. If we could not share the rational conviction that God has revealed Himself in the Bible and that what we believe as Seventh-day Adventists is supported by the Bible, we would find the church and its fellowship lacking in meaning and purpose.

Among the biblical teachings that Adventists hold, and that are especially important to us, are the Sabbath, the second coming of Jesus, and the wholeness of human beings. We see all these not only as scriptural teachings, but as integrally related to the most important doctrine in the Bible — salvation by faith through God's infinite grace revealed in the life, death, resurrection, and continuing ministry of Jesus Christ.

The Sabbath is God's generous invitation to spend one day out of every seven in a special time of fellowship with Him, with our families, and with our fellow believers on the anniversary of His creation of our world. This special time reminds us that God is both our Creator and our Redeemer. As we worship Him, we acknowledge that He is our Creator and Lord. Our very willingness to recognize His authority and bring ourselves into harmony with His law aids us in making Him the Lord of our lives. How can we possibly acknowledge Him as Lord and refuse His gracious invitation to spend this time with Him?

The Second Coming is God's gracious promise that Jesus has not only forgiven us and given meaning to our present lives, but that He has even more in store for us. We look forward to a time when all evil, suffering, and death will be brought to an end. There is so much uncertainty and threat to the very existence of human life in our world today that many are despairing. What will the future bring? Can our world survive, or will it go out with a

We are grateful to be part of a community of believers that takes the Bible seriously. As we study God's Word, we find hope for the future.

nuclear bang or a polluted whisper?

We are grateful to be part of a community of believers that takes the Bible seriously and believes that it does have answers to these questions. As we study God's Word, we find hope for the future. That is what it means to us to be *Adventists*.

It is also important to us to understand that we are whole persons, not immortal souls inside mortal bodies. This motivates us to give care and attention to every aspect of human life — both ours and that of others. Adventists recognize that not only is spiritual well-being important, but the physical, intellectual, emotional, and social aspects of our lives are important as well.

These three scriptural teachings — the Sabbath, the second coming of Jesus Christ, and the wholeness of human beings — are but a few examples of many important biblical teachings that we believe Adventists emphasize in a special way.

Our conviction that our religious beliefs are based on the Bible is primary among our reasons for being Adventists. But if our spiritual experience were only a matter of doctrine, it would be very empty. The attractive genius of Adventism lies in its ability to see the relevance of these important biblical beliefs for actual life.

Biblical teachings cannot be just cold, lifeless doctrines to be believed. They are God's helpful, gracious instruction designed to lead us to a better life now and forever. Seventh-day Adventists have recognized this and made their faith a way of life. What we appreciate most about being Adventists is the total way of life that we experience as we fellowship with others who share our convictions and lifestyles.

John

For example, the Sabbath is not just a doctrine, but a

special experience that our whole family enjoys together. That time at sundown on Friday night when we gather to welcome God's special day by singing, reading the Bible, and praying is a highlight of the week.

Several years ago I had to spend a few weeks in South Africa, halfway around the world from the family. It was that Friday sundown hour when the feeling of homesickness was the most intense. Fortunately the feeling was eased by fellow Adventist Christians who invited me to their home and let me join them as they welcomed the Sabbath in a similar way. This Sabbath experience has a special power to bind both individual families and the broader church family together.

An Attractive Wholeness

Some of the other aspects of this Adventist way of life that we especially appreciate are based on the biblical understanding of the wholeness of human life. This leads to an emphasis on healthful living and freedom from such harmful substances as drugs, alcohol, and tobacco, and to a whole system of education that emphasizes the harmonious development of body, mind, social relationships, and spiritual commitment.

If Adventism were only a set of doctrines, it would be cold and lifeless. And if it were only a lifestyle, it would be shallow and would lack credibility. What we enjoy about our church is the interrelation of belief and lifestyle into an attractive whole that makes sense and is relevant.

> *Biblical teachings cannot be just cold, lifeless doctrines to be believed. They are God's helpful, gracious instruction designed to lead us to a better life now and forever.*

Fringe Benefits

Now about those fringe benefits that we mentioned earlier. Both of us feel very grateful when we look at the ways we have personally benefited from the Adventist way of life. We are grateful, for instance, for Adventist higher education. It not only gave us a good education that served us well when we went on to graduate studies but also provided a setting in which we could meet each other and begin our married life and new home with someone who held the same basic values and convictions.

Both of us appreciate the church's influence on our children. They are both in graduate school now. Our son is married (to a wonderful girl he met at an Adventist college) and is studying to become a teacher and writer. Our daughter is studying psychology and is training to be a therapist. The present focus of her internship is on caring for emotionally disturbed children. One can never predict what one's children will eventually become, but we are very pleased with both of them and feel that the church was a positive influence during their formative years in shaping their values.

Ione

I also think of the special blessing that the warm fellowship and family atmosphere of Adventism have been for me after being alienated from part of my family. The words of Jesus have come to have special meaning for me: " 'I tell you the truth,' Jesus replied, 'no one who has left home or brothers or sisters or mother or father or children or fields for me and the gospel will fail to receive a hundred times as much in this present age . . . and in the age to come, eternal life' " (Mark 10:29, 30). I can truly say that the joy of fellowship in the church makes this promise a reality.

A Special Family

As we consider all these benefits, we stand in awe at the wonder of God's love and the blessings that He has provided. We firmly believe that He has worked in our lives and led us, through very different paths, to be Seventh-day Adventists.

When the Adventist Church held its worldwide business session in New Orleans in 1985, our whole family was able to attend. We joined with other Adventists from 184 different countries. We saw them carry their flags and wear their different styles of clothes. We met new friends and visited with people from several different cultures. As we celebrated the Sabbath together in worship and listened to voices raised in praise to God, we felt a bond that transcends nationality, race, age, language, and all other human barriers.

Not only was it an inspiration, but it also renewed our conviction that God has a plan for us and that His leading us to this special family, the Seventh-day Adventist Church, whose fellowship we gratefully enjoy, is an important part of that plan.